P9-DGB-401

FOCUSED ON THE TOP

Exclusive limited edition printing of
six hundred fifty copies, of
which this is copy number

GEORGIA TECH'S CHAMPIONSHIP STORY

Jack Wilkinson

LONGSTREET PRESS
Atlanta, Georgia

Published by
LONGSTREET PRESS, INC.
2150 Newmarket Parkway
Suite 102
Marietta, Georgia 30067

Printed in the United States of America

1st printing 1991

Library of Congress Catalog Number 91-061932

ISBN 1-56352-008-7

This book was printed by R. R. Donnelley & Sons, Willard, Ohio. The text was set
in ITC Clearface Regular by Typo-Repro Service, Inc., Atlanta, Georgia.
Jacket design by K Modack.
Book design by Jill Dible/Audrey Graham.

Photo credits: Louie Favorite, Michael A. Schwarz, Marlene Karas, John Spink,
William Berry, Frank Niemeir, Jonathan Newton, Kim Smith, W. A. Hodges,
and Joey Ivanesco of the *Atlanta Journal-Constitution;* Ron Hoskins; and the
Georgia Tech Athletic Department and Sports Information Office.

chapter 1

"Georgia Tech 1990 National Champions"** — the phrase first truly entered the public consciousness in the final minute of the Florida Citrus Bowl. The words flashed up on the scoreboard in an arena which had been dressed in white and gold all afternoon, as more than 40,000 Georgia Tech fans ushered in the New Year and rekindled an old era. And they reveled in the culmination of four arduous, at times agonizing years, too often hell but about to turn heavenly.

Indeed, since Bobby Ross' arrival on The Flats in 1987, he and his team had endured so much: a litany of adversity and antipathy, injury and indifference, ridicule, defeat and death. Yet by the time they'd reached the Citrus Bowl on January 1, 1991, Ross and the Yellow Jackets had not just passed through a four-year mettle detector; they'd thrived. And by New Year's Day, these were full mettle Jackets.

Against Nebraska, one of the proudest names in college football, Georgia Tech was as golden as its headgear, as brilliant as the Florida sunshine that day. From the opening moments, the Yellow Jackets dominated, then humbled the Huskers. In the final minute of that 45–21 triumph, the Citrus Bowl scoreboard proclaimed:

Georgia Tech 1990 National Champions.

Imagine that. Just 15 months earlier, the Jackets had gone nearly 2½ years without so much as an ACC victory. And now No. 1 was up on the board and in their grasp.

Affirmation — so unexpected and, thus, so much more cherished — wouldn't come until the next day. Yet no one who saw that New Year's Day display could dispute Tech's worthiness. Certainly, the Jackets themselves weren't about to.

"National champs! National champs!" safety Kevin Peoples chanted on the field as the clock wound down to 0:00. The turf was engulfed by thousands upon thousands of Tech fans, swarming out of the stands and tearing down first one goalpost, then the other. Linebacker Calvin Tiggle and defensive tackle Jerimiah McClary picked up Peoples' chant. And soon, it became the peoples' chant.

"National champs! National champs!"

Bobby Ross had already taken his celebratory Gatorade bath, the sticky stuff poured over his unsuspecting head in the waning seconds. Earlier in the day, Ross had stood on that same sideline and, thinking of his gravely ill mother lying in a Virginia hospital, told her, and himself, "Just hold on, I want to get there."

Martha Ross would hold on and her son would get there. But not before he was hoisted aloft at game's end and swept across the field. And not before he returned to Church Street Station in downtown Orlando—where he'd once faced such indifference—to receive the Citrus Bowl trophy and the adoration of thousands.

Then it was Shawn Jones's turn, lifted up and carried onto the field. Sometimes, shoulderpads make the perfect throne. It was Jones who had elevated his game, and his team, to another level that day, who had done so in characteristic fashion: humbly, shrewdly, completely. And magnificently. Without him, the game's—and the Jackets'—most valuable player, who knows how the scoreboard might have read?

Ross realized this. "Shawn, don't ever change," the coach told the quarterback on the field. "You're wonderful just the way you are."

As a seer, Ken Swilling ain't too shabby himself. "Told you so," the free safety had said to Ross after the regular-season finale, a 40–23 gouging of Georgia that left Georgia Tech the nation's only undefeated team. OK, so Swilling was only half right about North Carolina; that 13–13 tie was the lone blemish on Tech's 10–0–1 regular-season record. So what? The Jackets had gone

Citrus Bowl scoreboard says it all.

unbeaten, as Swilling had predicted—a prediction that drew raised eyebrows and snickers in August but looked positively psychic in January.

"It would be an injustice if we beat Nebraska and didn't get No. 1," Swilling said after the Jackets' win left them 11–0–1 and the Huskers reeling. "Regardless of the Notre Dame-Colorado result."

But then, this was hours before Rocket Ismail ignited the Orange Bowl drama that made even his draft-day signing seem tame.

"We're the only undefeated team in the country," said Jones, his logic as impeccable as his performance. "We should be No. 1."

Even Ross, until now loathe to lobby for votes, hit the campaign trail immediately after his team had riddled Nebraska for more points than any bowl opponent in Husker history. "As far as I'm concerned, it's settled," Ross said. "What did Colorado beat [Nebraska] by, 15 points? We beat them by 24.

"There you go," decided Ross, proving that occasionally, even coaches—especially those with national championships at stake—are as momentarily addled by comparative scores as the rest of us.

"I'll root for Notre Dame, but I think it should be settled by now," continued Ross, returning to reality. "We're the only undefeated team in the country. I don't know what else we can do. I feel we deserve it. I really do."

So, apparently, did enough other coaches. That wasn't apparent or official, however, until the final UPI poll of coaches the next afternoon. And it was fitting that the coaches honored Ross and Georgia Tech. Not because the coaches know more about football than do sportswriters. But rather, the coaches may have better grasped not only how good Tech had become, but how much it had overcome.

Throughout his Tech tenure, Ross had always stressed the notion of "focus." To focus on the entire self, the long range, on life beyond football and college—but all the

while focusing on the task at hand. In the 1990 season, that meant the weekly task, not the grail at the end of a Citrus-streaked rainbow. Somehow, through all the trials and frustration, heartache and tragedy, no one—players, coaches, support staff, no one—had ever lost sight of that focus. They'd not only retained it, they'd refined and sharpened it until now, they were focused on the top. And in a few short hours, which seemed unbearably long and hopeless at the time, they would finish focused on No. 1.

✳ ✳ ✳

"Fortunately," Homer Rice said, "sometimes I have instant instincts that trigger me like this."

Those instincts were never more acute, accurate and essential than they were on January 2, 1987. Rice and his wife, Phyllis, were driving to Florida, bound for a few days of vacation on Marco Island. But the Georgia Tech athletic director was preoccupied with developments in Atlanta, where his football coach, Bill Curry, was considering an astonishing offer: to become the new head coach at Alabama.

Never mind that Curry's overall record at Tech was an abysmal 31–43–4, nor that he had no ties with Alabama. Joab Thomas, then the Alabama president, was determined to stress academics in the post-Bear days in Tuscaloosa, and he was infatuated with Curry's commitment to academics.

On Friday night the 2nd, the Rices pulled into a Holiday Inn on I-75 in Gainesville, Florida, to spend the night. Rice spoke with Curry that evening, and again the following morning. At 8 a.m., Rice got a jolt of a wakeup call. At that particular Holiday Inn, the worst surprise was no surprise: Curry was leaving Tech to take the Alabama job.

How could he not? Even Bobby Dodd, the legendary Tech coach for whom

Ross aloft after Cirtus Bowl win.

JACK WILKINSON

Curry'd played, had advised him to accept Alabama's offer. Tuscaloosa was one of those rare outposts offering college coaches the chance to achieve the ultimate in coaching. Of course, that would prove the ultimate irony. When Curry left Tech and took his entire staff with him to Alabama, a major reason they cited was this: At Alabama, it's possible to win the national championship.

After talking to Curry, Rice checked out of the motel and headed toward Marco Island. Rice asked Phyllis to drive. He had to find a new football coach, fast. All his files were in his office in Atlanta. Rice pulled out a legal pad and pen and started jotting down the qualifications he'd seek in a coach, one who could pass muster with the Georgia Tech Athletic Association board. Then he started listing names, coaches from Rice's days in the NFL and in college. The answer came quickly, unexpectedly.

"All of a sudden," Rice recalled, "I thought . . . Bobby Ross. Where is Bobby Ross?"

Rice immediately asked his wife to pull over at the next exit. With trucks and cars barreling by on I-75, Rice picked up a pay phone and dialed Bob James, then the Atlantic Coast Conference commissioner.

"Bob," said Rice, "tell me about Bobby Ross."

Rice was familiar with Ross, knew all about the three ACC titles he'd won at Maryland from 1982-86. In the wake of the Len Bias basketball tragedy, however—and sensing a lack of support and unfulfilled promises of improved football facilities—Ross had resigned. He'd already taken a job as an assistant with the NFL Buffalo Bills. James told Rice that Ross was due to start work in Buffalo on Monday. In two days.

Undeterred, Rice figured he had two things working for him. In Atlanta, Ross would be a head coach, not an assistant. And at Tech, Ross would be living in Atlanta, not Buffalo.

"Is there anything there?" Rice asked James. Rice conceived the concept of The Total Person at Tech, one in which Tech strived to develop an athlete's total self, not just his bench press or time in the 40. He'd never heard any negatives regarding Ross, but wanted to make sure. As Rice remembers, "Bob James said he's the finest football coach he's ever worked with in his time. He's above reproach on any compliance problem."

Indeed, Ross's teams had not only played imaginative, high-scoring, winning football, their graduation rate was nearly as higher than his .672 winning percentage. Satisfied, Rice immediately called Ross's home.

Purdue and California had also courted Ross then. Both were turned down. When Rice reached the Ross residence and first spoke to Ross's wife, Alice, he was encouraged, even though Ross wasn't there.

"She was excited," Rice said. "Going to Atlanta sounded a lot better than going to Buffalo."

Rice drove on to Marco Island. There, he got a call from John McKenna, a former Associate Athletic Director at Tech and Ross's college coach at Virginia Military Institute. McKenna was proposing what Rice was thinking: Bobby Ross.

That evening, Ross called Rice, who explained he hadn't even had a chance to sound out Tech's athletic board. "If you're interested in the Georgia Tech job," Rice told Ross, "I'd like to go ahead and recommend you."

Ross was interested. One problem: he was due to start his job as Buffalo's quarterback coach and, Ross said, "I don't like to go back on my word."

Rice understood. He called Bills' head

coach Marv Levy, an old friend. Levy understood and said he'd have to talk with his general manager. The GM, alas, didn't understand. If Ross so much as talked to, much less visited, Tech, he was finished in Buffalo.

Rice and Ross talked some more. Ross understood. Rice talked to his faculty representative at Tech, then to interim president Henry Bourne, stressing not only Ross's credentials as a football coach but his integrity and commitment to academics. Convinced that the president and board were behind him, Rice persuaded Ross to fly to Atlanta sans guarantees.

"If they do not accept my recommendation," Rice joked to Ross, regarding the board, "then we'll both be looking for a job."

As Ross flew to Atlanta, the Bills broke the news that he was interviewing at Tech and finished in Buffalo before he'd even started. Rice met Ross at Hartsfield International Airport and drove him to the president's home. While Ross waited upstairs, Rice met the board downstairs. The vote was unanimous. Ross was accepted. He met with the board around 5 p.m., then two hours later was introduced at a press conference as just the eighth head football coach in the institute's history.

"To find a man of Bobby Ross's caliber that quickly, and go to work, well, he never even slowed down," Rice said. "He's a workaholic. He came right in and worked around the clock—and he hasn't stopped.

It's amazing how that all happened. It's not the norm."

Rice was convinced that the Tech program was such that an established coach could come in and take it to a higher level. Curry had led the Jackets to a 9–2–1 record in 1985 and a victory over Michigan State in the All-American Bowl, Tech's first postseason appearance since 1978. In '86, the Yellow Jackets finished 5–5–1 and blew a Bluebonnet Bowl bid when they lost their penultimate game to Wake Forest.

Still, Curry's departure initially crippled Tech, for several reasons. The timing was costly, smack in the midst of the recruiting season. And when his entire staff accompanied Curry, Ross inherited no coaches with contacts with recruits.

"What I didn't know was the year before turned out to be a poor recruiting group," Rice said. "We'd been to the All-American Bowl and didn't capitalize on it. Plus, we lost a lot of kids [to academics] the next two years."

Then there was the difference in philosophy between Ross's staff and Curry's. Ross was far stricter, far more demanding. Initially, many players chafed under those restrictions. And then some players, at first defiant, openly rebelled.

"I could see the frustrations," said Rice. "Here you have an established coach who knows how to win, and our program should have kept going. But we didn't have the players, the talent to keep it going. And the character was different. A lot of kids from the '85 team were great leaders, with real character. And they were gone. The new kids weren't the same."

Indeed, the new kids on the block, tackle and post pattern sorely tested Ross—to the point that they nearly drove him not only away from Tech, but out of coaching.

chapter 2

The Bobby Ross era dawned statistically spectacular if patently unrealistic. In his debut as head coach at Georgia Tech, the Yellow Jackets opened the 1987 season at home with a resounding 51–12 rout of The Citadel, as usual game but outmanned. The following week, before a capacity crowd in Grant Field, Tech astonished even itself by bolting to a 20–3 half-time lead over North Carolina. Late in the third quarter Tech was poised for the clincher, first and goal at the Carolina one.

In horror, Ross watched as Malcolm King fumble. Carolina recovered at the two, quickly scored on a 93-yard bomb and then rallied for a 30–23 triumph that left Tech badly shaken.

"I often wonder," said Homer Rice, "if we punched that in, where our program would've been."

Who knows? Had King scored, the Yellow Jackets probably would have beaten North Carolina and might have truly believed in

themselves. More likely, though, Ross's baptismal would have ended a 3–8 atrocity instead of a 2–9 disaster. Things were that bad on The Flats.

When Bobby Dodd retired from coaching after the 1966 season, he left behind a legacy of greatness as a coach and humanitarian. He took with him an era, an aura

Ross congratulated by Citadel coach after his first win.

and any hope Tech had of continued football success. In 22 seasons under Dodd, Tech won 165 games, lost just 64 and tied 8. The most cherished ticket in Atlanta on a football Saturday afternoon was a seat in the haughty West Stands of Grant Field. From there, Atlanta society watched Dodd—sitting on a folding chair at midfield, dashing in suit and fedora—orchestrate his teams with an intuitive, homespun genius. Tech teams were usually smaller than the opposition, usually better prepared and always better coached. Dodd cared for his players, treated them well, and they responded accordingly. Major-league professional sports hadn't come yet to Atlanta, but Atlanta had long since come to embrace Tech football, the only game in town.

From the 1950 finale through midway in the '53 season, Tech was unbeaten in 30 straight games. The '51 Jackets went 11-0-1, including a 17–14 Orange Bowl triumph over Baylor on a last-minute, wobbly, feeble field goal by Pepper Rodgers. That was the first of six consecutive major bowl triumphs in six years by Tech, which was then a national record and earned Dodd the nickname "The Bowlmaster."

In '52, the finest team in Tech history went 12-0, routed Ole Miss 24–7 in the Sugar Bowl and won the International News Service national championship. In the AP and UPI polls, the Jackets finished No. 2 to Michigan State. Tech opened the '53 season with four wins and a tie before losing 27–14 at Notre Dame, the eventual national champion.

During the '50s, Georgia Tech was the epitome of the modern college football program. The Jackets beat hated rival Georgia eight straight times and Dodd was lionized as the gentleman coach of college football. "In Dodd We Trust." "Dodd is God." He created the aura of The Tech Man, the palace guards, tackles and backs of The Flats. To start at Tech, much less star, was to be among the chosen. Professional football was hardly an appealingly lucrative profession, so many of Dodd's players remained in Atlanta after graduation and became wildly successful businessmen.

By the time Dodd quit coaching, though, much of that had changed. Tech was no longer a member of the Southeastern Conference, having left in a dispute over scholarship limits. The Jackets would flounder as an independent. They were no longer the only game in town, either. Professional football and baseball had come to Atlanta in 1966 in the form of the Falcons and Braves. The NBA Hawks would soon follow. With the advent of the AFL, the NFL was compelled to pay players more. Integration was coming to Southern college football. Tech was still stuck with a demanding curriculum that included the bane of the recruiter: calculus.

And then there was the loss of Dodd himself, of his commanding presence, his football intellect and his extraordinary good luck. Dodd's Luck, they called it. Without Dodd, though, Tech's luck quickly soured. From 1967-86, Georgia Tech went through four head football coaches and untold anguish. In those 20 years, the Jackets managed just nine winning seasons, never more than two in succession. They won nine games in a season but twice and, despite the proliferation of bowl games, went to just four bowls. Grant Field fell into disrepair and attendance plunged save for the occasional, traditional big-game rivalries like Georgia, Auburn, Alabama, later Clemson after Tech joined the ACC and, in the '70s, Notre Dame.

Neither Bud Carson, Bill Fulcher, Pepper Rodgers nor Bill Curry came close to rekindling the Dodd era. Attempting to do so seemed folly. Publicly—first as athletic

Legendary Georgia Tech coach Bobby Dodd.

director, then later as a consultant to the Georgia Tech Alumni Association—Dodd professed faith that someone—Rodgers, Curry, someone—could again win big, and consistently, at Tech. Privately, he dismissed the notion completely.

Into all this stepped Bobby Ross in 1987. Far from intimidated by Dodd's enormous, lingering shadow, Ross was intrigued with coaching at Tech, with Dodd still peering down from his private box in Grant Field. As a young high school coach, Ross revered Dodd's success and his methods. One of the first books on coaching football that Ross bought was a primer by Dodd. Ross was inspired by Tech's rich tradition, not intimidated by its recent failures, when he came to The Flats. Quickly, that all changed.

"When we first arrived here," said George O'Leary, Tech's defensive coordinator, "I thought it would be a long stretch just to get the people and players to be competitive in the ACC. I think defensively there were some kids that could play, but I think offensively, they just didn't have any

size or skilled athletes that could stretch the field for you, as far as make people defend the passing game and not crowd in on your running game. I think that's where we really improved ourselves most, the speed on the offense itself.

"In recruiting, you're trying to get people that can fit slots in your schemes offensively and defensively. When we first got here, though, the first two years, we were taking athletes, period. We didn't have the luxury of saying, 'We need three linemen, we need four of this.' When you're 2–9 and 3–8, you've got to take the best athletes available and try to make do with it."

Try to make do with this: In his first spring practice, Ross lost his best back for the season. Jerry Mays, perhaps pound-for-pound the best back in the nation in the late '80s, shredded a knee in the spring of '87 and was lost for the season.

Try to make do with this: Aware of Tech's stringent academic requirements, Ross didn't realize some players' academic deficiencies until it was too late. Between his

Under Bobby Ross, Joe Siffri learned all about hard work.

arrival at Tech and his debut against The Citadel, Ross lost nine players as academic casualties.

And try to make do with this: Hindered by a late start in recruiting, the loss of Mays and players flunking out right and left, Ross found himself faced with open defiance by many players and an outright insurrection by more than a few.

"I probably was one of his worst enemies when he first got here," said Joe Siffri, who'd just finished his freshman season when Ross arrived. "I rebelled against everything he said."

Siffri and several other players were rebels without a clue. They defied Ross simply because he wasn't Bill Curry, whom they'd come to Tech to play for, whose methods were so dissimilar to Ross's.

"Me and a couple of guys, we missed meetings, skipped workouts," said Siffri. "I guess we were just testing him. We figured if we couldn't have our own coach, one we came to play for, we thought we'd get him to do things [Curry's] way."

"A Southern-Northern thing," Siffri called the Curry-Ross dichotomy.

"There's two ways to skin a cat," said George O'Leary, "and they were used to skinning it the other way."

"Coach Ross is more disciplined because of his military background [Ross graduated from VMI and his first head coaching job was at The Citadel]," said Siffri. "Coach Ross had a schedule. You play good, you play bad, you stick to a schedule."

Siffri and friends had another agenda, though. "We'd be late to this, wouldn't put 100 percent effort into that," he said. "Let's say it was a 7 a.m. meeting. We'd wake up and say, 'We're really tired. Let's sleep a little longer.' We just didn't know what it was to work hard."

Eventually, they would. Eventually, they would work hard, grasp Ross's message and

see its fruition. But not before so many harrowing times, so much frustration, heartache and tragedy.

The 1987 season really unraveled in late October. The Duke week. That's when Riccardo Ingram, Tech's best player that year, was declared ineligible, having illegally signed with an agent. Saturday afternoon in Durham only magnified Tech's troubles.

On Halloween, Georgia Tech was humiliated by Duke 48–14. It wasn't just the 34-point margin of defeat that galled Ross, nor the fact that Duke—coached by Steve Spurrier, once an assistant at Tech, later an applicant for the head coaching job and a spurned candidate who vowed never to lose to Tech—was passing till the bitter end. Ross was appalled by Tech's lackluster effort and the awful realization that he simply wasn't reaching his players. For the first time, Ross pondered quitting. Not just Tech. Coaching.

"Humiliating," Ross recalled that day. "I can take the bad losses if you play hard and do your best. I just didn't think we were doing that."

At game's end, the message flashing on the scoreboard in Wallace Wade Stadium only heightened Ross's anguish:

"Welcome to the Basement, Tekkies."

"You want to know something funny about that game?" asked Kevin Bryant, Tech's director of marketing and promotions. "Bobby picked up more fans that game by being Bobby. It was a late game and coincided with the 6 o'clock news and a lot of TV stations did remotes of Bobby. He came out of the dressing room—that little bitty, lousy dressing room—and the bus was right there, and he came up and leaned up against the bus, and he kept saying, 'I'm sorry, I don't know what else to do. I apologize. I hope you forgive me.'

"That's all he kept saying. He was pitiful. But you know what? More people saw him on TV that night and said to themselves, 'Here is a guy that's putting everything he's got into this.' I had more people tell me that they became a Bobby Ross fan that night when they saw him on television, because they realized this was his whole life, this was his heart and soul.

"He's got that hat sort of tilted over to the side, he looks like hell, and he just kept saying, 'I'm sorry. I don't know what else to tell you, I'm really sorry.' "

Kevin Bryant, Tech's director of marketing and promotions.

Not nearly as sorry as Tech looked two weeks later, though, in a 33–6 drubbing by Wake Forest in Atlanta. "He almost quit after that game," said offensive coordinator Ralph Friedgen. "We all had to talk him into staying."

That night, distraught and seemingly devoid of ways to reach his players, Ross hit the road. First he and his wife dined in the parking lot at a Wendy's. After driving Alice home to Buckhead, Ross started circling I-285. Around and around the perimeter he drove, listening to Christmas carols and thinking, thinking, stopping only for one of his favorite foods: ice cream. Ross kept driving, kept thinking, kept eating ice cream. For awhile, it seemed Baskin-Robbins might run out of flavors before Ross ran out of gas and nervous energy. Finally, he pulled off the perimeter and returned home, feeling renewed and recommitted. He would need all the renewal and recommitment he could muster.

"You've got to realize he went through another year of that," said Bryant. "Another whole year."

chapter

Even before Ross's 1988 encore got off to a stumbling, bumbling, if victorious start, the Tech football program suffered a tragic loss. Tight end Chris Caudle drowned at home in Alabama while fishing in the off-season. The Yellow Jackets boarded buses for the trip to Caudle's funeral, where, locked arm-in-arm to support and comfort each other, they tearfully sang the "Ramblin' Wreck" fight song at the cemetery. It was the Jackets' first real tragedy under Ross. It would not be their last.

In the '88 opener at newly-christened Bobby Dodd Stadium at Grant Field, Tech nearly ruined the christening before awakening for a 24–10 win over Tennessee-Chattanooga, a Division I-AA school. That performance helped set the tone for the season. The Jackets were offensively deficient. Losing was ingrained in their collective psyche. Victory was elusive; of Tech's three wins in '88, only one came against a

Division I-A program. And that 34–0 upset of previously-unbeaten South Carolina was nothing to build on; the Jackets lost four of their final five games to finish 3–8.

"When I first got here, things were very different," said Willie Clay, a freshman cornerback in 1988. "After my freshman year, I never thought that we would reach what we did this past year. I couldn't imagine it. I mean, my first season was 3–8. That was very difficult for me because I was the new guy on the block. And I played my freshman year, I didn't get redshirted. So, I was thrown into the fire. Nothing against the older guys that were here, but a lot of them didn't accept me because they thought that they should be playing, and this and that. That happens every time someone new comes in.

"The problem with that team was, there was some talent. It was the same talent we have here now basically. Maybe not on

Marco Coleman prepares to hit USC quarterback.

JACK WILKINSON

offense, but we had a lot of talent on defense. But the players just didn't get along. Everyone had a me-me instead of a team-type thing. I believe that hurt us. I never played for a team that was that selfish before. I'm used to winning all the time. When you win, you can't be selfish. Truthfully, in my eyes we were selfish. That led to big problems in '88."

An even bigger problem erupted in the off-season: the infamous pizza brawl in January, in which offensive tackle Mike Mooney, guard Jim Lavin and linebacker Kevin Salisbury were involved in an altercation with a young woman (a Tech architectural student) and her boyfriend at an off-campus pizza parlor. Insults were exchanged and threats made that led to a fight, leaving the woman with a broken nose and the players facing criminal charges. Ross initially placed all three players on probation. Mooney and Lavin pleaded guilty to disorderly conduct and were fined; Salisbury pleaded no contest to a simple battery charge and was fined and put on probation. Ross later suspended Mooney and Lavin for the spring quarter and spring practice for violating their probation. They were reinstated in July amid much public criticism of Ross, who dealt fairly with the players and situation. Salisbury sat out a three-game suspension before returning against Maryland.

To this day, Mooney expresses not only remorse but also contends the full story was never presented in court or in print. Nothing better crystalized the furor surrounding the incident than a bedsheet banner that suddenly appeared one day hanging from the roof of an architecture building on campus:

The only thing that Tech can beat is women.

The banner, which hung for several hours before being removed, represented the feelings of many — not just toward the incident, but toward Georgia Tech football in general. It was no longer just indifference, but often outright derision. Indeed, the image and aura of The Tech Man was long gone.

"You felt so isolated," said tight end Tom Covington, a redshirt freshman in 1988. "You were very dogged when you lost. People wrote things on the wall: 'You stink. You might be around the corner and you'd hear, 'They stink, they can't beat anybody.' It was a terrible feeling that day with that banner.

"And you couldn't get anybody to come out for football games. Or, they were gone by halftime. I guess you couldn't blame 'em, but my feeling is, 'We're with you when you win, with you when you lose.' Well, they weren't.

"It was just hard to say, 'I play football for Tech.' It was like, 'So?' It was just hard to swallow."

It was hard not only for those who played, but those in waiting. By 1988, Ross was able to redshirt nearly his entire freshman class, who spent the season on the scout team, preparing the varsity for games and preparing themselves for the future. Many of those freshmen redshirts, however, wondered if they'd have any future on The Flats — including the kid who would become the most crucial cog in the 1990 national championship machine, Shawn Jones.

"My freshman year, when we were 3–8, I thought, 'What have I gotten myself into?'" said the quarterback. Playing on the scout team, Jones saw firsthand that Tech had good defensive talent but little offensively. Come game day, he remembers, "It seemed like the defense played 44 of 60 minutes."

Jones was not the only one who noticed that imbalance, and the indifference, if not hostility, toward football on campus. He wasn't the only freshman who considered an alternative: transferring. "A lot of guys talked about leaving," said Jones. "But I thought, 'We've got a chance. We can take over this program.' "

They had, and they would. But not before yet another miserable start, and another crisis for Bobby Ross.

When the 1989 season began, Georgia Tech had a new starting quarterback in Jones, who had spurned Georgia for Tech primarily because Ross had promised him every opportunity to play quarterback, not shift to another position. Jones's mobility was a refreshing change, bringing a new dimension to Tech's offense and putting new pressures on opponents' defenses.

"When Shawn came in, it added a more well-balanced offense," said Covington. "It put more variety in our offense. We had speed there that wasn't there before, and a person who could just tuck the ball and run. In the past, if we didn't get the pass off, that was it."

But while Jones was mobile, bright and determined, he was also young and inexperienced. And Tech was still Tech, mired in a whirlpool of despair and defeat. It would be a month before the Jackets' turnaround tangibly began. Once they turned the proverbial corner, though, they did so with tires screeching and never looked in the rear-view mirror. Those images were too many, too painful. Too recent, too.

The '89 opener was encouraging. Playing in Raleigh, Tech played a good North Carolina State team tough before losing 38–28. Back at home, the Jackets played a good Virginia team tough before losing 17–10. Then came the infamous Hurricane Bowl. In the wake of Hurricane Hugo's devastation, Tech traveled to Columbia, S.C., to face a South Carolina team bent on revenge. Hugo had ravaged the state and the Jackets found themselves holed up in a

hotel with no electricity or air conditioning. The game conditions were even worse. The Jackets bumbled their way to a 21–10 defeat. They were 0–3, and Ross was on the verge of quitting. Again.

Kevin Bryant: "Bobby and I were the last two people to get on the plane. We were out on the tarmac, and he says, 'Alice and I have talked about it, and we think it's time to hang it up. We just couldn't get it done.' I told him, 'You're crazy, just stupid. These three games are behind us.' And I really felt that, felt that we'd played pretty well in those three games. I said, 'This is a new season.' And he said, 'Well, I appreciate everything you've done for us. But sometimes, you just can't get it done.' "

Many of the players were despondent, too. Jim Lavin recalls thinking that, when Tech dropped to 0–3, "Well, we're not that good and maybe we never will be. Maybe we're not meant to win."

Homer Rice, though, also felt Bryant's optimism. But unlike Bryant, who'd never played football, Rice's faith was founded in his years as a head coach at Cincinnati and Rice and with the Cincinnati Bengals. Even the previous year, flying home from another disheartening defeat at Wake Forest, Rice had approached O'Leary and offensive coordinator Ralph Friedgen on the team plane with words of encouragement.

"George and I were like, 'When are we ever going to win a game?' " said Friedgen. "We were suicidal, about ready to slash our wrists. And here's Dr. Rice, coming back to see us. He says, 'I see us getting better. You guys can't get down. We've got some athletes here for a change. It can only get better. We said, 'Who is this guy?' It was kind of funny. I said to myself, 'Here's the AD trying to pick us up. Normally, he's trying to fire us.' "

"I could see Bobby's frustrations," said Rice. "Here you have an established coach

Tech students show their allegiance.

who knows how to win, and our program should have kept going. But we just didn't have the players, the talent to keep it going. But having been there myself, I could see Bobby's methodical approach, to develop each phase of the game. On defense, putting the defensive line together, the linebackers, secondary. On offense, the offensive line; he started recruiting big people, then skill people — running backs, receivers, then quarterbacks.

"He required strict class attendance, and really changed that around. And character — he really got on them about character."

Still, despite Rice's faith, the numbers were undeniable. Once, Bobby Ross ruled the ACC. Now, he'd lost 16 consecutive conference games and had beaten just one Division I-A opponent in nearly 2½ seasons on the aptly-named Flats. For a man so devoted to his craft and his players, Ross was doubting himself. And so were others.

"I think people in positions like mine — presidents, people in the selection process — they give up too quick," said Rice. "If you find the right person and he can't get it done, you've got to look at yourself: 'What can I do to help him?' There

was a thought that maybe Bobby doesn't fit Georgia Tech. Maybe he had some doubts at first. But I never saw a man who fit more than Bobby Ross. He was perfect for it."

And yet three games into his third season, Ross was still mired in defeat. After the loss to South Carolina, Georgia Tech had a week off before Maryland came to town. In those two weeks, three important events took place:

1) Ross's offensive and defensive staffs evaluated each other.

2) Ross and his players had a memorable meeting the Wednesday after the South Carolina game.

3) Ross met with three influential Tech alumni the following Saturday.

With a week off, Ross had his offensive and defensive assistants analyze each other. "We looked at each other and we had the defense tell the offense what they thought they saw from a defensive viewpoint, " Ross said. "And we had the offense look at the defense and tell them what they thought they saw from an offensive standpoint. I'm talking about not only structures — which we felt we had a good structure — but personnel, and how we were using our personnel. And we made a couple of minor changes after that in the way of using our people."

And one major change. George O'Leary felt the Tech offense needed to run the option more often, and also give the ball more to Jerry Mays. Friedgen agreed and decided, "If we're going to lose, we're going to lose with the ball in Shawn and Jerry's hands."

"And we worked very, very hard on a couple of things coverage-wise," said Ross. "We worked hard on our pass rushing."

But they weren't too hard on each other. Thorough, yes, and honest, bluntly so. But not divisively. For that, credit Ross, but also O'Leary and Friedgen.

They aren't just colleagues but close friends. Not just friends but neighbors who live on the same street in Marietta, three houses apart. "But I don't know if the neighborhood is claiming us," Friedgen said, grinning.

Most days, they carpool to work. Even in the bad times, during the losing, when either the offense or defense played well only to see the other unit blow another ballgame, they never blamed each other. And their rule never varied: one guy got to bitch until they reached Delk Road. Then, it was the other guy's turn until they hit Tech, or home.

"I think it helps the situation that George and I are good friends," said Friedgen. "You don't feel a lot of offense versus defense. I guess it hadn't been that way here, or something. Bobby promotes that, too, and that makes for a good working relationship. I've been on staffs where it hasn't been that way and people are always pointing a finger. We're all trying to work our butt off to win a game. It's not a question of somebody not working in this outfit. Some days you got it, and some days you don't and you've gotta find it.

"I remember our first year here, well,

George and I give each other a bunch of crap. We'll compete against each other pretty good in scrimmages and what not, but then afterward we ride home together and probably play golf together. But that first year, we got in the car and one of the writers from the *Journal-Constitution* said, 'I've never seen two coordinators laughing and joking all the time.' And I said, 'We're on the same team.' "

Some of the Jackets, though, were still not on the same page as Ross, not even after 25 games together. Ross had been encouraged by some things in that South Carolina loss: a semblance of a pass rush and indications that Tech was finally beginning to assert itself on the line of scrimmage. But the following Monday, after a sloppy start to practice, Ross called a halt and ordered everyone inside to the team meeting room. He was livid, and not just about practice. He'd received some lists, names of players who'd missed classes, Sunday study halls, weight lifting, late workouts. He'd had enough.

"Look, I'm getting tired of this," Ross told his players. "It isn't worth it to me. We've worked very hard to get to this point as a team and I think we're a pretty good team physically and about ready to be a good football team. And I think I know what I'm talking about. But I am tired of being a Gestapo agent. I'm telling you to get to the weight workouts, to get to class. Those things are as important to me as winning football games. They're important to winning football games. You don't win doing things this way, I don't give a damn how good you are. And it's no longer 'I'm gonna get you.' I'm gonna wipe the slate clean, but if you're not gonna do it, let me know.

"Now you sit in here and hash it out and decide what you want to do. If you don't want to do it and if you can't do it, then let

Defensive coordinator George O'Leary on the sidelines.

me know and I'm gonna leave. You don't even have to worry about me getting on you. I'll leave now, or I'll finish out the season and we'll work hard on the field and you can kind of do what you want to do. But I'll leave, and you'll know I'm leaving."

"He didn't feel like he was reaching some of us and that some of us didn't care," said defensive tackle Jerimiah McClary. "If it was better for the Institute, he'd resign that day."

"I was dead serious," said Ross. "I was fed up with it."

Ross left the room and the players took over. Specifically, senior noseguard Jeff Mathis, who said he was disgusted with everything: the losing, the lack of commitment, the overwhelming sense of gloom and impending defeat that hung over Tech like a perpetual mushroom cloud.

"Jeff said the problem was right here in this room," said Jim Lavin. "And the problem wasn't our ability, but our mindset. There was a show of hands. There were some that didn't know what direction to take. But the majority of us wanted to push on through this, with Ross and his staff, and try to turn this thing around."

Kevin Battle remembers: "There was a time then when Coach Ross was, like, 'You guys don't trust me. I get this feeling. And I told you I'd make you guys winners, but I can't do it if you guys don't respect or trust me. So, I'll leave you guys alone; all the coaches leave. If you want me to quit, just stick with me this season and then I'll leave.' We said, 'No, coach, no.' He left and the team got together and said, 'This is a coach who really cares for us, truly wants us to succeed and has our best interests in mind.'

"You know, most coaches just want you to play for them. I noticed that when I was being recruited by other schools. But Coach Ross not only wants you to play for him, but

Assistant coach Danny Smith signals in an offensive play.

he wants you to learn about life, college, to graduate from school. His main interest is getting us to graduate, moreso than playing ball, which some people may not believe or find hard to believe, but it's so true. He jumps down harder on us for missing classes and study hall than he would practice or a meeting. That shows a lot about his character.

"We weren't used to his honesty policy. Other guys talked to me about it, 'cause I wasn't here with the other coaches. They said they weren't really used to his policy for honesty and for making us go to breakfast and this, that and the other. And all that was to get us up, 'cause if you've got enough strength to get up, walk over and get breakfast, then you'll have more strength to go to class. Not a lot of people were used to that. It was hard, we would fight it. But we told him, 'We want you, we're going to trust you, we want you to

Anthony Rice exults.

stay.' Jeff Mathis came up to him and said that we needed to play for ourselves as much as the coaches. And from that moment on, there was a new commitment, 'cause we saw inside of Coach Ross, that we had a coach who really cared for us. A suspicion was there, but we didn't know it. But now we knew that he cared for us as individuals, not as cattle. It came out like that, and from that moment on, we won. We started rolling. That moment was the turnaround. That's what turned the season around."

In truth, it turned the entire program around and eventually led to a national championship. But even after that vote of confidence, Ross was leery when three prominent Tech alumni requested a closed-door meeting with him on the open Saturday morning between South Carolina and Maryland.

"I was a little concerned," Ross recalled. "Actually, I'm thinking, 'Well, I wonder if this is it? Maybe they want to tell me that they want to fire me.'"

Indeed, there was some real grumbling from some influential alumni going on. But that wasn't what Taz Anderson, Randy Carroll and George Broadnax had in mind at all. They wanted to reassure Ross, to reinforce their support of his program. And they wanted him to spill his guts.

"It was like, 'What's been going on?'" said Ross. "And I did. I kinda told them that. After it was all over, they said, 'Look, we're representing the [Georgia Tech Athletic Association] Board and want you to know that we're supporting you.'"

Armed with this vote of confidence, a new-found mutual self-respect and a productive self-evaluation, Ross, his assistants and his players promptly charged into Bobby Dodd Stadium the following Saturday and . . . fell behind Maryland 14–0.

The Terps scored twice in the second

With the Maryland game, everything came into focus for Shawn Jones and Georgia Tech.

quarter, the second time just 1:12 before halftime. In the next minute, the maturation of Shawn Jones truly began.

"In '89, at first it seemed like, 'Dang, what do I have to do?' " said Jones. "It seemed like I was out there and learning, I couldn't learn and then make mistakes. It was like I was out there in the fire."

But down 14–0 to Maryland, the flames licking at his heels, Jones suddenly became fireproof, and foolproof. His teammates, too. "When it was 14–0," Jones said, "a lot of guys got ticked off, like, 'This is ending right here.' "

Several Jackets also got extremely territorial. Jerimiah McClary and others conjured up a pep talk Homer Rice had given the previous year the day before the South Carolina upset. In the old Heisman Gym, Rice praised the coaching staff and the latest artificial turf surface, installed in 1988 and finally paid off in '89. The Jackets

recalled Rice's words: "This is our home field, our turf, and no one's gonna come in here and win." Before the pivotal '90 Maryland game, the week's slogan became: "No one's gonna come in our backyard and win."

And no one has since, the Jackets becoming college football's pre-eminent homeboys. But at first in their backyard, the Yellow Jackets — again — looked like yard dogs. Trailing 14–0, though, the Ross resurrection of Georgia Tech football began. In just 54 seconds, Jones drove the Jackets 69 yards in six plays. He completed five of six passes, the last an 18-yarder to Terry Pettis for a touchdown. It was merely an appetizer.

Never mind that Maryland scored quickly after intermission, after Willie Clay muffed a punt at the Tech 5. The Terps couldn't keep up with Jones' third-quarter airshow. In just over 10 minutes, Jones threw three

JACK WILKINSON

more TD passes: a 9-yarder to Tom Covington, a 5-yarder to fullback Stefen Scotton to tie it, then—after Jay Martin recovered a Maryland fumble—a 26-yarder to Covington for a 28–21 lead. Jones had become the first Tech quarterback in 17 years to throw four TD passes in a game.

Maryland had to settle for a fourth-quarter field goal after a TD-saving tackle by Swilling. On the game's final play, Swilling and Clay swatted away a pass to preserve Tech's first ACC win since Nov. 1, 1986. Finally, it had happened.

"And it kept happening," said Rice. "From that point on, we've lost only one game. And there's not many schools who could claim that, no matter who they're playing."

"That," said Jones, "turned everything around."

The goalposts come down after the win over Maryland, Tech's first ACC win since 1986.

The residuals—confidence, commitment and victory—were startling in their immediacy and degree. The next week, on the bus ride to Clemson, Kevin Bryant sat beside a slumbering Darryl Jenkins. The offensive tackle slept almost the entire way but not before telling Bryant, "You know, we're going to kick the hell out of Clemson."

That was 14th-ranked Clemson, a 20-point favorite and offering up Tech as a homecoming hors d'oeuvre to 82,500 in Death Valley. Still, Jenkins was extremely confident. "He felt like it may not be a close game," said Bryant, "and, . . ."

"The Play" against North Carolina.

And it wasn't. Tech stunned Clemson, winning 30–14. Jones was superb again, throwing for 223 yards and two scores. But it was the next week, back home in Bobby Dodd Stadium, that Jones grew up even more. Down 14–10 to an underdog North Carolina team, Jones dropped back to pass, evaded pressure, then scrambled 30 yards for the winning TD in a 17–14 triumph. On The Flats, that has become known as The Play.

Tech's only defeat since the Hurricane Bowl occurred the next week at Duke, when the ACC co-champions prevailed 30–19. The Jackets responded with resounding routs of Western Carolina and Wake Forest. Then, in an unknowing preview of 1990, freshman Scott Sisson kicked a 35-yard field goal with 42 seconds to play and Tech—with Swilling grabbing three interceptions — held off Boston College 13–12.

Jerry Mays made his last collegiate game his best. The diminutive tailback rushed for a career-high 207 yards and Georgia Tech rallied for a 33–22 victory over arch-rival Georgia. With that, Mays had the third-highest rushing game in Tech history and, with 1,349 yards, Tech's second-best single-season total. Mays concluded his career with 3,699 yards rushing, passing Eddie Lee Ivery and finishing second only to Robert Lavette. Mays joined Swilling and linebacker Eric Thomas as a first-team All-ACC selection. Jones, meanwhile, who passed for 1,748 yards and 12 TDs and ran for 330 yards and three more scores, was named ACC Rookie of the Year.

Perhaps the lone disappointment for Georgia Tech in 1989 was the lack of a bowl bid. The Jackets finished 7–4, 4–3 in the ACC, but finished out of the bowl picture. Many players were upset. Many fans, though, felt a new-found sympathy for the Jackets, especially after Georgia, only 6–5 and a decisive loser to Tech, received a Peach Bowl bid to play Syracuse. In early December, during the Georgia-Georgia Tech basketball game at The Omni, Bulldog fans bellowed their traditional "Go, Georgia Bulldogs!" cheer. Tech responded in parody: "Go to the Peach Bowl!" Georgia went, and lost. Tech went home for the winter, disappointed but determined and renewed. And quietly confident.

Jerry Mays scores against arch-rival Georgia.

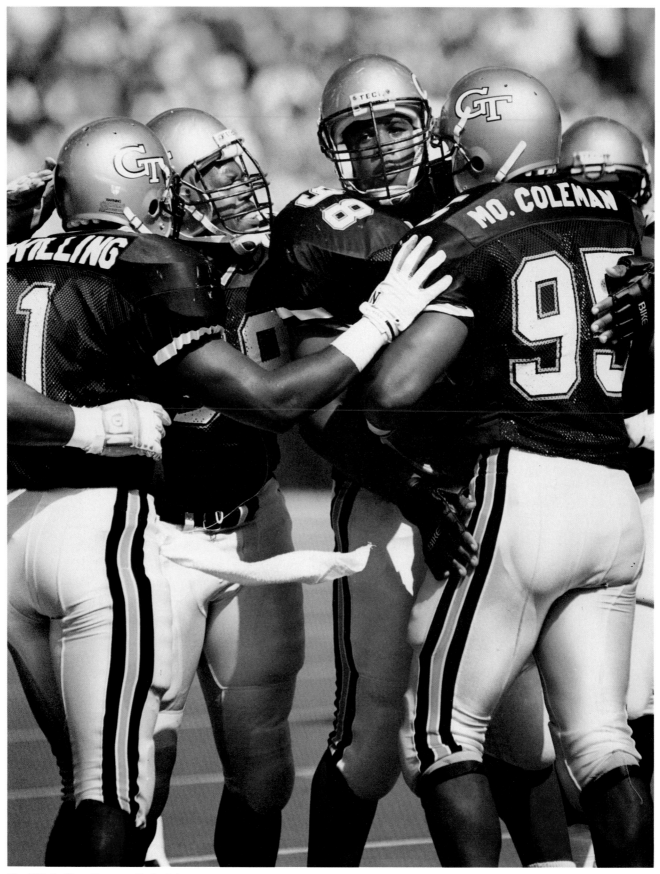

The "D": Swilling, Simmons, Battle, Coleman.

JACK WILKINSON

chapter

"I think we all had something to prove," said Mike Mooney. "I think that was the bottom line."

At Tech—or at least in the '80s, since Bobby Cremins' arrival—most folks had been far more preoccupied with the foul line than the goal line. Georgia Tech basketball, once the ACC's ultimate stepchild, had become the fair-haired boy on The Flats. With good reason. In March of 1990, Tech won its second ACC Tournament title under Cremins, then advanced to its first Final Four, losing to eventual NCAA champion Nevada-Las Vegas. In basketball, Tech was entertaining and successful—two things Tech football wasn't. Tech football players were friendly with, and supportive of, their basketball counterparts. Most were also highly envious. In the best sense.

"People were acting like Tech wasn't an athletic school, just a basketball school," said Mooney. "The basketball school thing

really got to a lot of us. We watched the Final Four. I was very happy for them. I went up to Tennessee for the NCAA game with LSU. We rooted for 'em. After it was all done, we heard all about 'Lethal Weapon' (the nickname for Tech's troika of Brian Oliver, Dennis Scott and Kenny Anderson). We heard how great those guys were. The whole school was just all in a basketball rage. We come in in summer ball and it was like . . ."

Mooney shrugged. Like, so what? No big deal. Fall camp's started in football? When's the basketball opener?

"The basketball team isn't any better than we are," said Mooney. "We've got just as good athletes. We've got Swilling, one of the best athletes ever, and Shawn. You tell me there's lots of schools with guys like that, I find it hard to believe. But I think that helped us. Basketball going to the Final Four really helped us last year. I really believe that turned the whole thing around here. We wanted some attention, too. Everybody wants it—positive attention."

Attentiveness, too. That is something Tech had in abundance in the summer of '90. Some 60 players spent the summer in Atlanta, many attending summer school, all preparing for the 1990 football season. In years past, players and coaches had pushed pumping iron and running and prepping for the fall. But that was so much summer and smoke, everyone trying to convince each other they were all on the verge of something good. But now, coming off a 7–4 season and winning seven of its last eight games, Tech felt it was on the verge of something great.

So they worked, the Jackets did, lifting together, running together in summer's heat and humidity. "In the middle of the day," Swilling recalled, "to get used to the heat and get more out of your bodies."

And they worked in memory of Dave Pasanella. A former Tech player in 1983 and '84, Pasanella had become the Jackets' strength coach. Along the way, he also grew to 6–0, 275 pounds with 21½-inch biceps. Pasanella became the premier powerlifter, earning the distinction of "The Strongest Man in the World." But in April of '90—the same month that former Tech basketball player Anthony Sherrod committed suicide—Pasanella was killed in a car crash near campus. At the intersection of Northside Drive and 10th Street, Pasanella's car was hit by another on Northside. His car hit a metal utility pole, killing Pasanella and sending the Tech campus into shock. Again.

"This comes as a terrible shock to us," said Ross, who would honor Pasanella by having his team wear blue football patches with white initials "DP" on the left breast of their game jerseys. "Dave was a fine person and coach. I don't believe in jinxes,

but a lot of terrible things have happened."

More were yet to come. But that summer, good things were happening, too. Shawn Jones ran with his receivers, all running together on the track inside Grant Field "and pulling for one another." More important, they also worked together on their passing game, working on timing, running routes endlessly until they were perfect, building on their 1989 success and—particularly with wide receivers Bobby Rodriguez, Emmett Merchant, Greg Lester and Jerry Gilchrist—laying the foundation for Tech's most improved position in '90.

There were great expectations on The

Jackets' strength coach Dave Pasanella.

Flats, the most since 1985, when Tech finished 9–2–1. Ross, though, had less lofty aims than many, hoping merely to win at least seven games. That would give Georgia Tech consecutive seven-win seasons for the first time since Bobby Dodd's farewell. Ralph Friedgen was hopeful of winning eight, "if things went right for us and we stayed healthy. I would have been very happy with a 7–4 season. If you are in the top 20 consistently every year, I think one of those years it all goes right and you're gonna have your shot at it all."

Which is exactly what Ken Swilling had in mind. On Georgia Tech's media day in August, Darryl Maxie of the Atlanta Journal-Constitution asked Swilling for a prediction for the upcoming season. Swilling's reply: "11–0 would be an excellent record. And it's very feasible."

Maxie rolled his eyes as Swilling spoke. Then Maxie sought out Bobby Ross. "Well, you know, . . ." Ross said, rolling his eyes, "that's a young man talking."

A very confident young man. And one who was not alone in his confidence. "If we're not 11–0, we'll be somewhere in the vicinity," McClary said that day, seconding Swilling.

As strong as they'd finished the previous season, as many starters as they had returning, the Jackets still had uncertainty on both sides of the ball. Offensively, Friedgen had to find a replacement for Mays and hoped his wide receivers would make big catches, not big drops. Defensively, O'Leary was leery of his line.

"We were worried because we lost all our linemen," O'Leary said. "The first five and six defensive linemen, they graduated. The only one back that played No. 2 was Jerimiah and Kevin Battle played sparingly. Beyond that, we had nothing. We're basically looking for people and we had some young kids, so the biggest concern was the development of the defensive line. I thought we were solid everywhere else.

"When we left spring ball, I thought defensively we had great speed, the fastest defensive club since I've been here. Just watching what we do, we just closed so quick around people that we just close like a spider jumping on everything, putting a web over it. I knew we were going to be pretty good, just lacking experience on the line. When the lights came on, I was waiting to see what those young kids were going to do. And they made mistakes. But they're all aggressive mistakes. I can correct that. It's those timid, what-the-hell-happened mistakes that get me in trouble."

In the O'Leary scheme of things, it was imperative that Tech's defensive line mature and produce quickly. His defensive philosophy is based on defensive linemen occupying as many blockers as possible, thus freeing up the linebackers to make the play. One of those new defensive linemen was tackle Coleman Rudolph, a sophomore and a converted stand-up defender. "On our team, the linebackers are really supposed to make the major defensive plays," said Rudolph, whose father played at Tech in the '50s and who opened the season at right defensive tackle. "If we don't do our job, then the linebackers are out." And the opposition is in Tech's secondary and the Jackets are out of luck.

Offensively, Friedgen was guardedly optimistic. "I thought we had a chance to be better than we were the year before," said Friedgen. And this despite losing Mays. "I was concerned about our tailback position. T.J. [Edwards] is a good player, but he just hasn't been healthy. I had a lot of confidence in William Bell, but I knew he was going to have to play with the responsibility which he hadn't. When he came in as a freshman, he was in a backup role, and he looked very good and had a good spring practice. He was going to be a good football player, but he was going to go through the freshman mistakes because he hadn't played in a big game. I think Jeff Wright was a pleasant surprise and Carl Lawson came on and played real well, played his best ball at the end of the year and that helped Stefen Scott at fullback. I thought we got tremendous mileage out of kids like Mark Hutto; the contribution he made made us a better football team. And Anthony Rice, too.

"For the first time, we started having

Emmett Merchant's TD versus Clemson.

JACK WILKINSON

some depth. We could throw eight receivers out there and they could play. Some of the kids that were our top receivers two years ago are now our fourth and fifth receivers. I thought our biggest improvement on offense was our wide receivers. They went from being our least productive players to our most productive players. For three years, our tailback has been our leading receiver. Now we have three wide receivers who have more catches than our tailback, and we are throwing the ball up the field more. They are making bigger plays. They are making more big plays than they are dropping the ball.

"That gave us such a shot in the arm offensively, because we didn't have to just be a possession passing team any more. We could be a team that could go for the big one and stretch out the field that way, which opened things up underneath and helped open our running game up, too. So for the first time, I felt like we had both ends of the spectrum. We could run the ball, we could throw it deep, we could throw it short, and now you've got a chance to really mix them. When you don't have that you're kind of limited. You've got one hand tied behind your back, and you can't . . . for the longest time, we couldn't attempt a long fly pattern. The field just shrunk. We were playing from hashmark to sideline. We are playing on a bigger field now. It's like having those three-point shooters in basketball. Nobody's packed in around you."

Packing it in was something Georgia Tech football hadn't been able to do in awhile. Attendance at Bobby Dodd Stadium had been low throughout Ross's first three seasons. That was always a point of contention with the coach. Especially when Tech's marketing slogan for football last year was, "Football is Back." When Ross heard that, Kevin Bryant recalled, the coach wanted to know one thing: "Where the hell's it been?"

"He still kids me about it," said Bryant. "Where was it? Well, it was down."

And so, correspondingly, was attendance. In 1989, when Tech began its current unbeaten streak with a win over Western Carolina, just 28,821 fannies sat in Grant Field. The next home game drew only 26,114 for Wake Forest and on a dark, chilly, Thanksgiving Weekend Saturday, just 28,221 showed up for Boston College. Those figures deeply disturbed Ross. So in the summer of 1990, he centered his standard speech to Tech booster and alumni clubs around attendance.

"It was tough for me to sit there and listen time after time about how disgusted Bobby was with the crowds," said Bryant. "But I understood. But I know people aren't going to come back after one good year. Still, he harped on it a lot. He gave figures. I don't think Bobby knows this, but it was real excruciating for me, because that's my cup of tea. That's what I'm responsible for. Bobby is responsible for coaching, I'm responsible for filling the stadium. Bobby kept saying to me, 'This has nothing to do with you, you know. I'm getting on them.' But it was hard for me to shake and really hard to take. But I understand where he's coming from."

On Sept. 8, 40,021 fans came to Bobby Dodd Stadium to see Tech's seniors start keeping their word. They'd vowed to beat every opponent at least once before leaving The Flats. North Carolina State was the first of three teams Ross had never beaten while at Tech. "A vendetta," Jerimiah McClary called this game. Play word association with the Yellow Jackets and when the words are N.C. State, the responses are: Hot. Nervous. Fumble. Hot. Defense. Hot. And hot some more.

Officially, the temperature was recorded at 91 degrees, with the on-field temperature a sizzling 105. Maybe the heat fried Thomas

Ramblin' Wreck drives onto field for 1990 opener.

Balkcom's memory; he recalls the temperature as 118 degrees, "the hottest game I ever played." And this from a guy from Miami. On the Tech sideline, four large fans and four air-conditioning units fought the good fight against the heat. And lost.

"I thought it was hot, but it was to our advantage," said Ralph Friedgen. Before the game, he was on the field, talking to an N.C. State assistant coach who asked, "Boy, does it always get this hot here?"

"What?" replied Friedgen. "This is just a normal day here."

"You're kidding me," said the N.C. State coach. "On this turf?"

"Oh," said Friedgen, "we practice like this all the time."

"I knew what was on their mind," Friedgen recalled. "I thought that was a good sign for us." Indeed, all those hours and laps in the summer sun would begin paying dividends for Tech. Immediately. Or as Jones said, "It was really hot, but we were in great shape."

Many in the crowd weren't, though. By the second half, dozens of spectators had passed out. In the third and fourth quarters, droves of fans — many women — were stretched out beneath the West Stands, trying to recover and stay cool. By then, N.C. State couldn't do either.

Ross felt the opener was crucial. Not in terms of national championship implications (it was weeks before he'd allow himself to have such thoughts), but rather, Tech was off the following week and Ross didn't want the Jackets dwelling on yet another season-opening defeat for two weeks. For Shawn Jones, the opener's significance was as tone-setter: "A game that could determine how we were and where we were."

So naturally, on Tech's first play of the year from scrimmage, in his first carry as a starter, William Bell fumbled at the Tech 26. "That really didn't bother me," insisted Bell. "I was upset because it was a fumble and we lost the ball, but I just couldn't let that get me down." The Jackets' defense stiffened, fortunately, and N.C. State settled for a 3–0 lead. So naturally, on his third carry as a starter, Bell fumbled again. "That fumble there, that kind of stirred me," Bell said. As he returned to the sidelines, running backs coach Danny Smith soothed Bell, told him to just relax. "And the rest of the team," said Bell, "came over and said, 'It's still early — but you've got to hold onto the ball.'"

While Bell mulled over that advice, T.J. Edwards replaced him. Bell suspected as much when he'd returned to the sideline and seen Edwards stretching. "If I were the coach, I know for a fact that I would have put him in, too. So, there was no hard feeling there." But there was a churning in Bell's stomach. After the game, he would allow that he'd had butterflies in his gut before the game. After his second fumble, "Those butterflies were pterodactyls."

Having fumbled the ball away on the first two possessions, Friedgen sought to calm his offense and his own jangled nerves. When Tech regained possession, he told himself, "Let me give it to Stefen. He's our senior fullback, a steadying influence here. Let's get it out of here."

JACK WILKINSON

"So he fumbles it," Friedgen recalled, "and they go for the touchdown."

Fernandus Vinson scooped up Scotton's fumble and the defensive back returned it 11 yards for State's only TD and a 10–0 lead. And upstairs in the Tech coaching booth, Friedgen is asking himself, "Now who the hell do I give the football to?"

Even that early in the game, that early in the season, Friedgen could breathe deep the gathering gloom and doom. "I think we were on the verge of panicking," he said. "Pat Watson [offensive line coach] and Danny Smith did a helluva job of keeping them in the boat and saying, 'Don't jump ship.' And, like what happened in so many games this year, we put Jeff Wright in and got something offensively."

It took awhile. Tech wasted a scoring opportunity when Willie Clay blocked a punt, only to see the offense stall again. "We were like, 'Just don't worry about it, we just gotta play ball,' " said Clay. "Now, if that had happened in my freshman year, and the offense hadn't scored, there would have been a lot of bitching going on. But nobody said anything. Everybody just went on and played."

Then Jones hit four straight completions, the last to Greg Lester, whose spectacular 23-yard catch and run cut N.C. State's lead to 10–7. Then, in the fourth quarter, it happened. "We exploded," said Jones. "That's something I had been waiting on."

First Bell caught an 8-yard scoring pass from Jones to give the Jackets the lead for good, then knelt in prayerful thanks in the end zone. Late in the day, Tech sealed the

Willie Clay blocks punt against N.C. State.

victory and flexed its physical superiority by driving 54 yards to score. Wright ran for all 44 of his yards, including a clinching, 9-yard TD with 2:49 left. For openers, for a change, Tech was 1–0 in the ACC.

Afterward, an N.C. State assistant told O'Leary that the Wolfpack might not recover for three games. It wasn't just the heat, but the physical licking O'Leary's defense had applied.

"He said they were just thoroughly beat up," said O'Leary. "So I think that game gave us confidence. It was a good win. It was the first time we had beaten them, they had a pretty decent team and it was an opening game for us. And that got a little bit more confidence up front for us. The kids hung in there very, very well as a unit. You can attribute that to Bobby. He's going to make sure they're all team players, and not any 'Me's' around. And that game and the whole year, we got good senior leadership. Jerimiah McClary, Calvin Tiggle, Jay Martin, they just did an outstanding job.

"I think you're only as good as your senior class. I don't care what your juniors or sophomores look like, if you don't turn to them for leadership. It's your seniors, and it has to be a senior that's playing, not a senior who's going to be riding the bench. That's where I thought we came from. When we first arrived, I didn't think we were very strong or quick, but I think the addition of that weight facility [an ultra-modern strength and conditioning complex in the Wardlaw Building overlooking the south end zone] has helped us tremendously. When we play other people, you can see there is a dominance in the line of scrimmage, one way or the other, and for the last 18 games it's been that way offensively and defensively. Even though we've gone against some bigger people, we've held our own. And it's coming out of that weight room."

Bell kneels after scoring winning TD.

JACK WILKINSON

chapter

Football players talk. Occasionally, opponents talk to each other during the week, before the game even begins. When the opponents are Georgia Tech and Tennessee-Chattanooga — an unlikely pair — they talk a lot.

"That game was real personal," said Jerimiah McClary. "We were talking back and forth all week on the phone."

The callers were familiar to each other. Tech's Keith Holmes has two cousins who play for UTC. Several of Thomas Balkcom's friends from his hometown of Miami play for the Moccasins. Kevin Burley came to Tech before transferring to UTC. All week, they all talked on the phone. Mostly, they talked trash, as players will. Burley and the Mocs were relentless in replaying their initial encounter in 1988, when Tech opened the season at home against the Mocs. For three quarters, the blitzing, gambling UTC defense confounded the Jackets and UTC

led 10–7. Finally, in the fourth quarter the Jackets righted themselves, asserted themselves and managed a thoroughly unconvincing 24–10 win.

This time, the Mocs brought the rain with them to Grant Field. It was a dreary day, and George O'Leary wondered how focused was Tech. "I think it's a money [large guarantee] game for UTC, and it's a game we're supposed to win," he said. "And as much as you tell the kids, no matter what person is coming in here as a team means they have the capability of beating you, it's still . . . you bring in a I-AA [team], it's tough to get that across to kids."

Not so Friedgen. "Chattanooga was a I-AA team but I thought their talent level was pretty good," he said. "I thought that game came at a good time for us. I thought our kids went in and played that game up, not down. Not overconfident. What I was happy to see was that Shawn was put into a situation where in the past, pressure had bothered him. Two years ago, when Chattanooga came down and just about killed us, they pressured on every down. Some of the things they do are really not sound, but they are rolling the dice. What do they care? They've gotta come down here and do it — and we kinda took them apart.

"I think it was a good learning experience for Shawn, because he was successful against pressure and burned them against pressure. I think he grew from that game."

So did his statistics. Jones threw for a career-high 265 yards, including a 78-yard scoring pass to Bell, and directed Tech to a 44-9 rout. Jones took control immediately, punctuating the Jackets' first possession with a 3-yard scoring run. "That set the tone," he said. "We went right down the field, even with them blitzing. We were going to see that all year, and see it until you prove you can beat it."

Jones proved it early, and often, and it was an invaluable experience. No matter the classification or talent of the opposition, it's always good to beat the blitz. And Jones beat it thoroughly: his 15 completions went to nine different receivers. Clearly, Tech's passing game was no longer Jerry, Jerry, Jerry.

Jeff Wright on the fly against UT-Chattanooga.

Just as clearly, Tech's passing game was no longer kaput when the quarterback was pressured and in trouble. On the second possession, Jones was blitzed and nearly sacked. But he eluded a tackle and scrambled right, then found Bell alone on the left sideline. "I don't know how Shawn found me," Bell marveled. "The guy was pulling him down, but Shawn got away and came up throwing and found me — and I'm his last choice on that and I was 15 yards down the field. He was almost 17 yards in the backfield and he just came up and found me and took two steps and threw it, and it was right there. And the rest was easy."

The rest of the day, too. Up 20-9 at halftime, Tech scored 24 unanswered points in the second half to win easily, if not aesthetically. "We won the game, but if we had played anyone that was really good that day, we probably would have gotten beat," said Clay. "It's games like that you need to make you realize that you have got to get things together even against a UTC."

O'Leary's critique of his defense? "Sloppy." And this despite forcing seven turnovers, including five interceptions — two by Marcus Coleman. "But as far as some of the yards and tackles," O'Leary said, "I thought we were bad there."

So bad, in fact, that O'Leary and his defensive aides didn't award the Big Stick — the shillelagh, or Irish walking cane, presented to the defender who made the best tackle, or hit. The 4½-foot-long stick, made of polished hardwood, was discovered by secondary coach Chuck Priefer three years earlier at Atlanta's Renaissance Festival. In bestowing it on a player, Tech's coaches were seeking to develop a defensive hitting mentality; in other words, walk softly and deliver a big stick. The defender honored would then carry it around campus for a week.

If O'Leary was loathe to award a Big Stick, so was his boss. "We played very poorly defensively," said Ross. "Offensively, we were kind of a hit-and-miss-type team. I wasn't particularly pleased with the way we played, but I wasn't gonna overplay it."

Indeed, Ross was determined to be a more positive Tech coach than he'd been upon arrival. "For the last two years, I've taken the approach that I wasn't gonna be negative," he said. "The first year, I might have. But that first year, my concern was just to get us to play hard. And we only did it about half the time against Chattanooga. I was more concerned about that, but I just kinda wiped it off. I just said, 'Look, it was a good win and we can play better. You know we can play better. Let's go on.' "

And after all, Tech had held to one of Ross's tenets for success: Beat the teams you're supposed to beat, and then win a few you're not supposed to win.

* * *

Matthew Levy said it best.

"The whole school's on a high," the Tech student and AEPi fraternity brother gushed in late September. "We had success in basketball and baseball. We got the Olympics. School's started and we're 2–0 in football. And I've got a teacher who looks like Meg Ryan."

Indeed, this was a high Tech campus: The Final Four in basketball last March. Then the baseball team was ranked No. 1 in the nation for a time. Then Juan Antonio Samaranch, president of the International Olympic Committee, said the magic word—"At-LAHN-ta"—and the 1996 Summer Olympics were not only coming to Atlanta but Georgia Tech would be the site of the Olympic village. And in the first week of classes for the fall quarter, the football team was 2–0 for the first time in six years

and only the second since 1970.

And now South Carolina was bound for Atlanta, 4–0 and ranked No. 25. ESPN was coming, too, to televise the 4 o'clock game nationally. It would be Tech's first national TV appearance in two years, since the desultory 24–3 defeat at Georgia in '88, and its first ESPN appearance since the 30–16 loss to Georgia in Ross's first year. But unlike those games, Tech was not merely a TV bit player this time. Indeed, the Jackets shared co-billing with South Carolina. All of it was new—or new again—to Tech.

Georgia Tech is back on TV.

"Those were things we had not seen in years—a full crowd, national television, a nationally-ranked team, a national ranking at stake," said Kevin Bryant. "This was something I had not experienced before, and it was great."

It was also a new experience for ESPN, which loved Tech's traditions: the great setting of Grant Field, Buzz the mascot, the Ramblin' Wreck, the student flashcard section. All that, and now a team that could play a little, too.

The student body sensed that, too.

Indeed, there was a campus-wide optimism that hadn't been this strong this early in the season in two decades. As gratifying as that felt, many Tech players—in particular, those out-of-staters who were from up north—were just as excited about another group of fans: those who'd be watching back home on TV.

"Every time you go home, everyone says, 'When are you gonna play on TV?'" said Tom Covington, a New Yorker from Hempstead, Long Island. "You say, 'I don't know.' Notre Dame is on TV all the time. This was our chance to shine."

"I'm from Pittsburgh and my family never really gets a chance to see me play on national TV," said Willie Clay. "So it was time for me to shine and show what I can do to a national audience. That's a big thing, and you're aware of it. I don't care what they say. You are aware of it going into the game, but once the whistle blows you don't care if anybody's watching, in the stands or on TV."

"I told my friends back home they could see me on TV," said linebacker Marco Coleman, who grew up in Dayton, Ohio. "If they didn't have cable, go to a friend's house. Playing on TV is a big deal for players like me whose parents live a long way away and can't get down for games. Plus, you feel like a star—if you play like one."

And Coleman did. He had lots of company, too. "This was a chance to make a statement nationally, that we're really good and can play with anybody," he said. "We played like national champions that day."

They played before a capacity crowd of 46,011. Many of them were South Carolina fans who came here anticipating a big weekend in Atlanta that included, naturally, another victory. And they voiced their optimism, early and vociferously. As early as the pre-game warmup. Coleman Rudolph vividly recalls lying and stretching in the end zone, directly in front of the majority of Gamecock fans.

"When you're in that end zone," Rudolph said, "and you can't hear the coach who is five feet away during warmups, then you know it's going to get loud again."

Shawn Jones also had a memorable pre-game warmup. Consequently, so did Ralph Friedgen. "I will never forget this," said Friedgen. As Tech warmed up, Jones dropped back to pass. He planted his right heel and . . . suddenly, Jones ripped off his helmet and flung it angrily to the turf. And he stalked off the field.

"Where are you going?" Friedgen cried out.

"It hurts like hell," said Jones, who kept walking toward the entrance to the locker room. Friedgen quickly summoned trainer Jay Shoop and said, "We gotta take care of him."

In the summer, Jones had bruised his foot, closer to the arch than the heel. He kept aggravating it and the pain began working its way up toward his Achilles tendon. In warmups, he planted the foot and felt something pop. "It hurt bad and sent a sharp pain up my leg," said Jones. "I thought I had broken something and was all upset. I was afraid I wasn't gonna be able to play all year."

In the training room, Shoop gave Jones a shot of cortisone. He came back out and played, but, as Friedgen said, "He didn't throw the ball well. He was kind of erratic, like he had been in the past. He couldn't plant his back foot, that was really part of his problem. He just didn't play well at all."

But then, he didn't have to. Defensively, Tech was the magnificent 11.

The Jackets scored first, Jones scoring on a one-yard, fourth-down option keeper to climax a 17-play (15 rushes), 88-yard drive.

The three Colemans: Marco (95), Marcus (27), and Coleman Rudolph (rear).

team," McClary said. "As far as our defensive scheme goes, the defense goes as the defensive line goes. So we had to prove ourselves early. We shield the offensive linemen so the linebackers can stay clean and make the plays. We filter all the plays to the linebackers. If we don't hold up the offensive linemen, then the linebackers are blocked and they're into the secondary and our whole defensive scheme falls apart."

McClary reminded his linemates about this, telling them, "Everybody's got us under the microscope that we're the weak link. I know deep down inside that we can compete. We've just gotta go out and prove ourselves."

"I just didn't know," McClary said, smiling, "we'd jell that early."

That early, and this well: Led by linebackers Jerrelle Williams and Coleman, Tech held No. 25 South Carolina to just 196 total yards, including a paltry 40 yards rushing. The Jackets were determined to shut down the Gamecocks' wideouts, then focus on the fulcrum of South Carolina's one-back offense: Mike Dingle, a big, bruising back. But not for long that day.

Dingle finished with only 41 yards on 15 carries, including a fumble. Dingle's miscue was one of five turnovers Tech forced that day. Swilling had two interceptions and O'Leary had a sense his defense was bound for glory, at least, if not greatness. "The kids swarmed the ball and they played defense," said O'Leary. "I thought South Carolina was where we started to come as a defense. Really, they played well and they knew they played well. But you still have to have that little edge where you say, 'We still did this wrong, or that.' Cockiness is one thing and confidence is another. But I thought South Carolina was a trigger game for the defense. They executed well, tackled well, they did everything that you're supposed to do."

Actually, Tech had to go 93 yards after an illegal procedure penalty. The Jackets led 7–0 and never trailed. Up 10–3 at halftime, Georgia Tech broke the game open on a two-yard TD run by Stefen Scotton that was set up by completions of 23 and 29 yards from Jones to Bobby Rodriguez. By then, though, O'Leary's defense had broken South Carolina's resolve, long before the final margin reached 27–6.

Afterward, Jerimiah McClary said, "We wanted people to know there was something going on in Atlanta besides getting the Olympics."

Before that game, McClary had held a little meeting with Rudolph, Battle and the rest of the defensive line. "We went in as the question mark of the whole football

Calvin Tiggle (58) and Jerimiah McClary (96) put the hit on Mike Dingle.

With the victory, Georgia Tech was now 3–0 for the first time since 1970. And the Yellow Jackets appeared in the national rankings at No. 23, their first AP ranking since 1985. "That's just about where you want to be," said Ross. "You don't want it to jump too soon because you start thinking you're better than what you really are. But it was a real confidence builder for us and I think afterwards, people started to say, 'Hey, this is a team that needs to be watched a little bit. They're not up there with the big boys, but they're a team that's coming.' So, it was a very productive game for us from that standpoint, and also that we'd improved our pass rush. I think that's been one of the most important things for us."

That pass rush would never be better than it was the next Saturday.

* * *

The Maryland game was significant on several levels. It marked a triumphant return to College Park for Bobby Ross. It showcased an astonishing, All-America performance by Marco Coleman. And it afforded all the Jackets their first celebratory flight home in the Ross era. When they landed, the Jackets were even more warmly received than when they'd left.

"There was starting to be a buzz around campus," Jerimiah McClary said. "People standing and watching us walk to practice. They were taking notice of the different things we were doing."

The Yellow Jackets dress in their locker room at the Edge Athletic Center adjoining Bobby Dodd Stadium. Then they walk several blocks through campus to the grass practice facility at Rose Bowl Field. They pass several fraternity and sorority houses, buildings belonging to various student groups and a couple of campus bus stops. In the past, they might as well have been invisible.

"We have a different color scheme," said McClary, referring to the various jerseys football players wear during practice: the defense in blue; offense in white; scout team in orange; injured players who couldn't practice in red; those who could practice but no contact in yellow; quarterbacks wearing blue pullovers atop their white jerseys so no defenders will hit them. "For three years, no one had taken notice of that," said McClary. "This year, people actually knew what the different colors stood for. That stood out in my mind: people actually realized that Georgia Tech had a football team, also. 'He's wearing red, he must be hurt.'"

As the Jackets trudged to and from practice, fraternity brothers would watch from their front lawns, or engineering majors from their bus stop. "It was just a different feeling than we had," McClary said. "People had never been concerned about Georgia Tech football. In the past, either they ignored you and made it blatant, or turned around and looked the other way. Now they were acknowledging us. That made a big difference."

Ross didn't make a big deal about his return to College Park. Tech, after all, had already played there once, losing 13–8 in '88. And Ross had already beaten the Terps in '89. Yes, he'd quit at Maryland with three years left on his contract. But no, this was no personal vendetta.

"At that point, it was just another game," said Ross. It was a conference game, it was a road game, our first road game of the year and that's why it was important — not because it was Maryland. See, it was more . . . to me, things had changed. We were focusing on winning because of what winning meant to us. It wasn't revenge. We were thinking beyond those things. If you're going for the conference title, you've gotta beat them."

And Ross wasn't certain Tech could beat the Terps, who were 3–2 but had lost to Clemson by a point and, in their fifth game, were within 21–17 early in the fourth quarter before losing 45–17 at Michigan. Ross felt "scared to death" of the Terps and their quarterback, Scott Zolak. Surely Maryland would have revenge in mind for that embarrassing (to them) loss at Tech in '89. Perhaps that's why the Terps taunted Tech on the field during pre-game warmups. The Jackets ignored them, then swarmed them.

Jones passed for 276 yards, a new career high. He was extraordinary that day, as were most of his teammates in a 31–3 thrashing of Maryland. "That," said Terp

Marco Coleman sacks Maryland quarterback Scott Zolak — again.

coach Joe Krivak, "is probably as good a licking as we have taken all season."

"We were a complete football team," said Ross.

As proficient as he was, though, Jones, like most everyone, was talking about someone else afterward: Marco Coleman. "I'm glad I didn't have to play against him today," said Jones.

"Marco Coleman was a monster," said Balkcom. "He was Maryland's worst nightmare."

A recurring nightmare. The Jackets had

11 quarterback sacks. Coleman had five of them—two shy of Pat Swilling's Tech record—and might have had at least another had Zolak not barely slipped out of his grasp once. Another time, Coleman flushed Zolak out of the pocket before making the tackle at the line of scrimmage. No gain, no sack. The 11 sacks helped reduce Maryland's rushing total to minus 20, a Georgia Tech defensive record.

"It was good coverage," was the explanation of the sacks offered by the 6–4, 250-pound sophomore. "That gives you more time to work moves and get to the quarterback. I give all the credit to Willie Clay, Keith Holmes, Thomas Balkcom and Ken Swilling."

Ross partially credited Tech's defensive preparation—helped, in large part, by Maryland's new offensive scheme. Like South Carolina, Maryland employed a one-back attack. "There was a tremendous carryover defensively from South Carolina to Maryland because they were nearly a mirror offense," Ross said. Plus, his Jackets were uncharacteristically emotional, even the day before the game. "Zippy," Ross characterized them. "I've never seen 'em as zippy and enthusiastic as they were." After the brief workout Friday, when Ross called the Jackets together, they were hollering, jumping up and down. "They never do that," Ross said. "I mean, they didn't even do that for the Citrus Bowl. To this day, I can't tell you what it was."

Scott Zolak could: it was Marco Coleman, the MC Hammer Ross dropped on Maryland. On the first play of the second quarter, Coleman recorded his third sack. Then the Terps adjusted, finally, and double-teamed Coleman. Still, he managed two more sacks and became a Coleman lantern lighting the way for the rest of the pass rush: the double-teaming he drew led to the other Tech sacks. All in all, not bad for a guy who had a bad cold that day.

"I couldn't breathe," said Coleman. "My nose was stopped up. I asked coach Shoop to give me something for my nose that wouldn't make me too drowsy. First play, I couldn't breathe. As the game went on, I felt better. As I started sweating, I felt better. I played real hard and ended up in the right place at the right time.

"This was the first game I got single-blocked. I just made it a point that if they were gonna one-on-one me, they weren't gonna block me. If a team single-blocks me, I say, 'Make 'em earn it.' We'll see how they block me next year."

George O'Leary knows they won't block him this way: "Their left tackle—Marco lined up on his side and must have beaten him about three or four times already. The quarterback started to check [off] a play and—I've never seen this before—Marco must have jumped and the kid started going back. And the quarterback, instead of calling the signals went to check a play. And the kid was going back and just fell flat on his back at the time the quarterback was snapped the ball. And that was one of the sacks. I thought it was a movie."

That Coleman was playing at all, much less so spectacularly, was the real wonder. During his first year at Tech as a redshirt, Coleman felt some pain in his stomach the week before the Georgia game. He suspected a pulled muscle. By Christmas break, the pain was so severe he couldn't get out of bed back home in Dayton. His mother sent him to a hospital where he was examined and operated on for a possible hematoma. Wrong. A second look revealed a ruptured appendix that had burst, then grown infected. Considering how long Coleman had carried the ruptured appendix inside himself, doctors told his parents Coleman was fortunate to be alive.

"I thank God for that," said Coleman,

A swarm of Yellow Jackets.

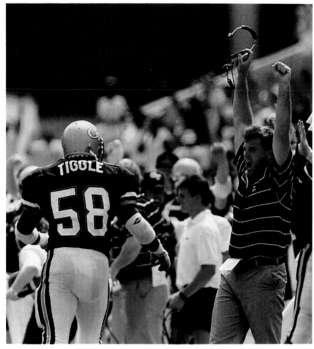

Calvin Tiggle and Tech had much to rejoice about all year long.

who lost 38 pounds during the ordeal but managed to work his way into the starting lineup for the '89 opener. "I know I was kept alive for some reason. I don't know what it is, but I know I'm supposed to do something."

For Tech, only one thing was better than the Maryland game itself: the flight home. For the first time under Ross, the Jackets flew home victorious on their Delta charter. Until then, Delta should have awarded Tech frequent crier miles. They loathed to fly, and it showed.

Remembrances of flights past:

Jim Lavin: "Awful. We'd stare out the window with gloomy faces."

George O'Leary: "Awful. You'd look out the window and go, 'I wonder how far it is down there?' Ralph and I always sit next to each other on the plane. It just got awful. It was the same pilot all the time — a Delta pilot named Bob Lewis — and the same stewardesses, including Jenny Kaiser (daughter of Tech basketball great Roger Kaiser). The plane was all decorated with Georgia Tech stuff and they tried to be so nice: 'You guys really hung in there real

good.' And you really want to jump off and go, 'Leave me alone.' But it was hard because they tried to be good about it, but it was never a pleasant trip home. You're always sitting there and looking at the drive chart and seeing what the hell happened as far as where were the major breakdowns."

Jerimiah McClary: "Coach O'Leary and Coach Friedgen would sit together solemn, like they were flying to a funeral."

Willie Clay: "It was always depressing coming home after you just lost. It could have been a two-hour flight, but it seemed like we were coming from L.A. or something."

Ralph Friedgen: "We fly great. Delta Airlines takes care of us great, better than any place I've ever been. They usually wait there for us, where other places, the plane has to come in and you are usually waiting there for the plane. They give us a filet mignon meal every time. It's a first-class travel situation. The only bad thing about it is, we never won. It was like being in some part of hell. You've got everything nice around you but you feel like crap."

Not this time.

"You'd think we just won the national championship," said McClary. "We were up dancing and singing. Even Coach O'Leary was up laughing and talking. That's weird to see him laughing and talking."

Even singing and dancing. As usual, McClary sat with Balkcom and T.J. Edwards. The trio began a chant: "I got a feeling — oh yeah! — it's in the air — oh yeah! — ..." And they would call upon other players, then coaches to get up and get down. Even the defensive coordinator joined in. Imagine that: George O'Leary, song-and-dance man.

Kevin Battle revels in the raucous memory: Card games, wrestling matches, peanuts flying through the air, players, even a coach or two dancing in the aisles, singing.

At last, singing at 30,000 feet. "Everybody was just going crazy," said Battle. "It was like a big bash, a big party. The stewardesses just stopped telling us to sit down. It was a wild time. After that, I thought Delta would never, ever ask us on their plane again."

Clay sat with his best buddies and traditional seatmates, Coleman and Calvin Tiggle. "The three amigos," Clay calls them. The fourth amigo, though, cornerback Marcus Coleman, was injured the previous Thursday in practice and lost for the season. His three good friends dedicated the rest of the season to Marcus, and all three inscribed "MC" on their football shoes. That night, though, the Jackets needed dancing shoes to come home in.

"That flight was the greatest feeling," said Tom Covington. "You can never remember coming home on the plane happy. There was always that gloom feeling, everybody down. But to actually fly home laughing and call home and say, 'We won!' was euphoric."

As euphoric as the Jackets felt—and felt they acted—Friedgen was somewhat surprised at their reaction. "I thought it was going to be a little crazier than it was," he said. "One of the things I used to love at Maryland was when we would win, our kids would just go nuts on the plane. They would take over the loudspeaker system. They would laugh and play jokes on everybody. Bobby would have to calm them down because they would be making jokes on the president's wife and stuff like that. Everybody was fair game. They would get on the coaches. But I like that. I like being loose like that, I like to raise a little hell myself. And our guys were pretty sedate. I don't know if they just haven't done that here, but I know I was happy. I think that's the only game George and I went out afterwards. We'd been waiting for three years.

Upon arriving home, the Jackets awoke on Sunday morning to find Furman Bisher's words in the *Atlanta Journal-Constitution,* under the headline, "The dawning of Tech's Bobby Ross Era." It was Bisher, longtime sports editor of the *Journal,* who had exchanged halftime hellos in the Maryland press box with ACC commissioner Gene Corrigan. "When did Georgia Tech become this kind of football team?" Corrigan had asked. "They are good. They are impressive." Bisher agreed.

"Prepare yourself, folks, and practice constraint at the same time," his column began. "This may be something here. This may be the football team Georgia Tech has longed for, dreamed of, fantasized about since the days of Robert Lee Dodd. The latter-day Bobby may have constructed a juggernaut. A powerhouse. A team of Killer Bees.

"This may be the start of the Robert Joseph Ross Era."

* * *

By now, it was clear that Georgia Tech was no longer rank, but ranked: No. 18 in the AP poll. And, to accompaniment of much amusement in many college outposts, ranked No. 1 for the first time in the weekly *New York Times* computer rankings. But how legitimate could such an antiseptic poll be? After all, Notre Dame had been ranked No. 1, but after a shocking 36–31 South Bend upset by Stanford, the Irish had tumbled to No. 30. Then again, maybe the *Times'* computer knew a little football after all . . .

Defensively, the Jackets were ranked, too. They were fifth nationally in overall defense, allowing just 224 yards per game; and third in rushing defense (62.5 yards per game), turnover margin (+2.25) and, most important, scoring defense (7.75 points a game). Which pleased George O'Leary immensely.

"The only statistic I care about is your scoring defense statistic," said the defensive coordinator. "That's the only one that matters. All those other ones are nice and they get you in the NCAA guide, but they don't get you anything as far as the wins and losses—because defense versus the score is the most important statistic. And that's what we look at. Boom! We're going to stress that."

A long-time Long Island high school coach and then Syracuse assistant, O'Leary can X and O with any defensive coordinator anywhere. His scheme includes multiple fronts and coverages. More important, though, is the essence of his football philosophy: Put the ball down.

"You win as a team, so I'm basically a 'Put-the-ball-down guy,'" he said. "I don't care where it is. I don't huddle up after sudden changes; to me, it's sort of ludicrous. You're playing defense and there's a sudden change and you're in a normal down, so I don't see huddling up right now 'cause there's a fumble out there. Let's put the ball down and play defense. That's why we practice, that's why you're on scholarship. Put the ball down, that eliminates all this, 'Damn, they turned the ball over again, they fumbled' type of deal. Put the ball down and give us a chance to show why we practice. How would you like it if you never got a chance to get out there, to play defense? And I don't care where it is; that's my job to make the calls [depending on] where it is, not for you to worry about it. Just play what's called.

"We talk two things: Put the ball down, and then make something happen in three downs. 'Make it happen in three,' we talk about. Go out there with the intention that we need turnovers. Don't just be content to

Inside linebacker Jerrelle Williams.

JACK WILKINSON

make them punt the ball. Get a turnover."

In other words, CPR. Club, punch and rip.

"CPR, that's a term we use for stripping [the ball carrier] drills," said O'Leary. "I'm big on initials. It's easier for me to go out and say, 'CPR!' on the sideline. They know what I'm referring to, our club, punch and rip techniques. 'Come on, CPR!' But a layman could look at it and go, 'Somebody down or what?' "

More initials: G and G-minus (number of times on the ground). L for loaf (not getting off the ground). K is a knock-back, getting knocked off the line. Unlike many coaches, O'Leary isn't consumed with grades, yelling at a player who graded out at 40 per cent of all plays in fulfilling his assignment. "If he's the best kid, he's still gonna play next week," said O'Leary. "But I'll say, 'Hey, you're on the ground 10 times out of 50, how the hell are you going to help us on the ground?' Then the kid can relate to what he's not doing: crossing his feet, playing too high, peeking in the backfield."

And when all else fails, O'Leary becomes a conventional defensive rubberband man. Bend, don't break.

"If there's a fumble and we get down there with the ball on the 3, three points is all I want to give up," O'Leary said. "There's a big difference. You fight your butt off, don't give up that seven. Let 'em make three. Just 'Put the ball down, let's play.' Always go back to it, and keep harping on it."

Leading up to the Clemson game, O'Leary also kept harping on this: Someone was finally going to score on his defense. So, no big deal. Don't worry about it. Just put the ball down — again — and keep playing.

Through the first four games, 16 quarters, the Tech defense hadn't allowed a touchdown. Eight field goals, but no TDs.

The lone touchdown scored against Tech was that fumble return in the opener. While some were enthralled with the scoreless streak, O'Leary wasn't going to turn it into a crusade. He is, after all, a realist. Especially when the next opponent is Clemson.

"Some of the coaches wanted me to [use the streak as a motivator] but I never did," O'Leary said. "I didn't have to. The kids knew. The papers wrote all about it. I may have mentioned it to them about the third game: 'No one scores.' But that bubble is going to burst at some time, and how you react to that bubble is, 'No fingerpointing, they scored, next time put the ball down and let's play defense.'

"If I started making a big point of that, all of a sudden you have guys trying to make plays instead of doing what the defense is supposed to be doing. And I think it's more important that it's a team-type thing. We won the game. If we held them scoreless, that's part of the win as a team. It's nice for the defense, but it's still, 'We won as a team.' If you start emphasizing that [streak] too much, you start separating things a little bit. And when Clemson did score, it wasn't like it was a big deal. You could see the kids were annoyed, but not to the point where you worry about, 'Well, they scored, we're going to fold our tent.' "

When Clemson finally did score, it demonstrated much about the Jackets' maturity. It also revealed their talent, and tenacity, and resolve. All of which Tech would need.

Mike Finn, Tech's assistant athletic director for communications, called Clemson "the toughest ticket since I came here in '83." Bobby Ross called Clemson something more:

"The biggest game we've played since we've been at Georgia Tech."

Al Ciraldo and Bobby Ross.

Check that.

"It wasn't a game. It was a war. One of the hardest-hitting games I've ever seen."

It was the first time since 1984 that two ranked teams met at Tech. Then, the No. 20 Jackets upset No. 13 Clemson 28–21. This time, a regional television audience, 17 representatives of 10 bowl games and a capacity crowd of 46,066 (Tech's largest since 1985 and the new stadium configuration in 1988) saw a remarkable game on a glorious day, one that was truly an Oktoberfest for Tech.

It began in the morning mist on Techwood Drive, as hundreds of Tech fans gathered outside the players' gate at Grant Field. They were part of a new, increasingly-popular tradition: Greet the Team. Among them was Kim King, Bobby Dodd's last quarterback, an Atlanta developer and real estate magnate and The Young Lefthander—Al Ciraldo's radio sidekick.

"We win today, it'll dramatically impact the program in many ways," said King. "The older people are getting excited again. The younger ones will always be excited. But the older people, the Dodd Era people, are starting to say, 'This is for real.'"

Not since 1966, when King was Dodd's sophomore quarterback, had Tech started a season 5–0.

Shortly before 10 o'clock, it was obvious that, literally and figuratively, the football bus stops again at Tech. To the shrill accompaniment of a squad car's siren, the two team buses pulled up. As always, the Jackets had spent Friday night at the Marriott Perimeter, then bused to the stadium after breakfast.

"At breakfast, a lot of the guys were real quiet," Thomas Balkcom said later that day. "Some of the younger guys were edgy. But when we got here, that really excited us that the crowd was behind us, believed in us, believed we had a chance to win."

The Jackets filed off the bus, silently, grim-faced. When the sidewalk crowd cheered and the Tech pep band blared away, just a few players smiled or high-fived. They filed through the old wooden gate, which was festooned with yellow flyers advising "Destroy Clemson!" and splattered with dozens of "5-0s."

The Varsity was as aromatic, and packed, as ever. And, seemingly, equally divided between Tech gold and Clemson orange. Indeed, gazing north, I-85 seemed a river of orange flowing south. Tiger fans tailgating on tables in the Varsity parking lot roared when a Clemsonized American flag passed by: orange and white stripes, with an orange pawprint on a blue background. T-shirts abounded, including a new model: "UN-BEE-LIEVABLE!" printed below Buzz the Yellow Jacket. Last year's post-Clemson biggie at the Tech bookstore: "The Death Valley Sting, Georgia Tech 30, Clemson 14, October 14, 1989." This time, Clemson was determined to turn any Tech garb into an all-wet T-shirt.

Over on Bobby Dodd Way, the air was redolent with the scents and sounds of a college football Saturday: Barkers' hot dogs grilling, music wailing and scalpers working the crowd. Quite well, too. An $18 ticket on the 50 was bringing as much as $100.

And inside Bobby Dodd Stadium, a passion play was about to unfold.

For Tech, Clemson would be an orange litmus test, a barometer of just how fitting were these Jackets. They all felt it, from Bobby Ross to Thomas Balkcom's father. They just didn't know the barometric pressure — even from Clemson — could be this intense.

It was Balkcom's father, J.T., who had told his son before the season even began that if Tech started 5–0, the Jackets "would go all the way." Undefeated? Still unlikely, perhaps, but no longer unfathomable. Not if

"Captain Bookbag": Stefen Scotton, Academic All-American.

Clemson fell. That would be anything but easy, though. Yes, the Tigers had dropped their opener, losing their first-ever to Virginia. But their defense was at least as staunch as Tech's; the Tigers were third nationally in total defense (199.5 yards per game). Their offense, evolving behind an outstanding line anchored by tackle Stacy Long, was averaging 283.8 yards rushing and 32 points per game. And this was, after all, Clemson, an opponent most teams dread.

Not Tech, though. Ross loves playing Clemson, particularly in Death Valley. He loves it all: all that orange, Tigers running down the hill after rubbing the rock, the 82,000 crazies who truly care about their team. He loves the big-time, big-game atmosphere there and loves preparing for, then competing against such a fierce opponent. Ralph Friedgen does, too.

"I love playing Clemson," Friedgen said. "I know it's going to be a hard-hitting, tough football game. It's going to be, 'Who's going to gut it out to win it?' You're not going to finesse it. I told our kids two years ago and told them again this time, 'Men, you've gotta beat Clemson. And you're not going to beat Clemson if you can't run the football.' They play the run very, very well. If you get away and you have to throw the ball all the time, then they just lay their ears back and you're going to have trouble.

"It's one of those games where a four-yard run looks like a great game. When you're in a good football game, you think this guy ran, like, 'What a great run!' You look up and it's second and six. You know you're in a game. All the great games I've been in — Penn State will be the same way — you're just happy to make four or five yards in the running game. But you've gotta have the pass. And I told them, 'When we have our opportunities, we can't let them slip through our fingers. When we get a turnover, we get field position, that's when you have to cash in.' "

The Jackets grasped the game's import, too. Clemson is perenially among the ACC's top two or three teams, and usually the best. A victory over the Tigers midway through the season — and this time, in a game in which Tech couldn't sneak up on Clemson — would legitimize the Jackets in many minds, including their own. And it would likely give them clear sailing to Char-

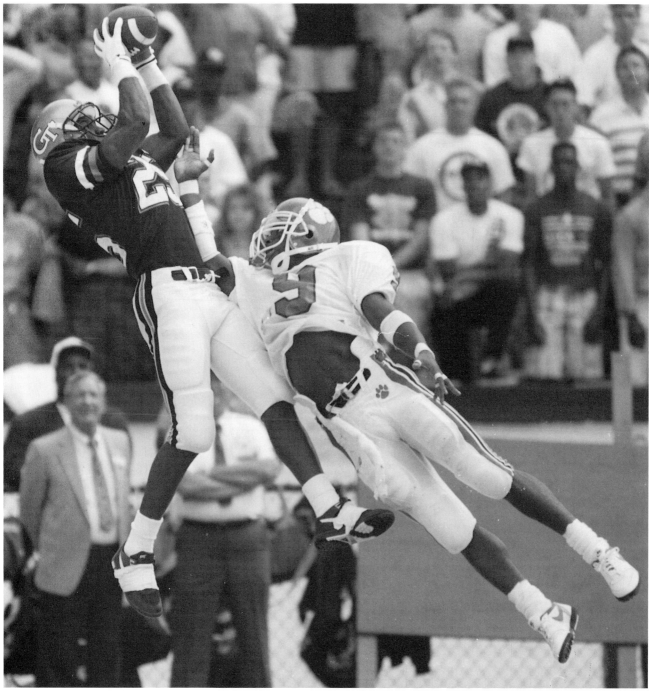

Greg Lester's spectacular catch against Clemson.

lottesville, for a showdown with Virginia.

Against this backdrop, Georgia Tech and Clemson painted a masterpiece. A bone-jarring, heart-wrenching, last-gasp master-piece. For Tech, it was an epic that dawned ominously.

Taking the opening kickoff, Ken Swilling lumbered up the left sideline. At the 30, in front of the Tech bench, he was slowed but not downed by a Clemson defender. "I was just gonna fall forward," Swilling said. "A guy grabbed me and I was trying to shake loose. He was holding onto it and was already down, and people fell on me and on him. That made my whole foot pushed almost flat on the ground. As soon as it happened, I knew it was hurt pretty bad."

On the sideline, Swilling told the trainers to tape it. "I still couldn't do it," he recalled. They loaded him on an electric cart and carried him into the locker room. No improvement. "I wasn't gonna come out," Swilling said. "But I thought about the game and where we were and who we were playing and I just couldn't stay in the locker room. I had to play."

When Swilling returned with five min-utes remaining in the first quarter, the crowd went bonkers and Tech seemed in total command. Jones hit Emmett Mer-chant for an early 7–0 lead. On Clemson's next possession, linebacker Chris Simmons sacked quarterback DeChane Cameron, whose fumble was recovered in midair by Coleman Rudolph at Clemson's 13. Follow-ing a 4-yard loss, Greg Lester adjusted his pass route and made a spectacular catch for a 17-yard TD and 14–0 lead. And then Bobby Ross reverted and became a Mary-land Terrapin again: a turtle who went into a shell big time.

Admittedly, Ross made "a very big coaching error in that game. I got too conservative."

It was an error that nearly cost him the game, but ultimately helped him win the national championship. Come the Citrus Bowl, Ross remembered his reticence against Clemson and vowed not to make the same mistake. That approach repelled Nebraska when the Huskers rallied. That approach might have made for a much shorter day for Tech's defense against Clemson.

"A doubleheader," George O'Leary called it. And indeed, for his defense, the second half seemed to last two halves that made a whole lot of high anxiety for Tech.

"Absolute hell," Willie Clay called the memorable, interminable third quarter. "A gut check."

"Totally frustrating, helpless," said Jim Lavin. "We couldn't do anything. I couldn't just run out there and try to play defense."

Up 14–3 at halftime, Ross told Ralph Friedgen to run the ball to open the third quarter. Keeping the ball on the ground, though, kept Clemson in the game. The Jackets couldn't run the ball against Clem-son's dominating defense. And they couldn't stop Clemson's powerful inside running game long enough to sit down and come up for air.

Just as they'd prepared, and hoped, for, Tech had contained Clemson's outside option attack. The Jackets' defensive speed was primarily responsible. In the second half, though, Clemson abandoned the option outside, used a two-tight end align-ment and started pounding away inside, isolating Tech defenders and allowing exceptional running backs to operate behind that awesome offensive front, run-ning leads and power sweeps. Early in the third quarter, Clemson controlled the ball for 17 plays, traveling 71 yards, but had to settle for a field goal after Calvin Tiggle made one of his 24 tackles that day, down-ing Cameron at the 3.

When Ross saw that, he wanted to eat up

the clock a bit. On such a hot day, he also wanted to give his already-tiring defense a rest. After asking how long that Clemson drive had lasted, Ross ordered Friedgen to do the tighten-up. Just one problem.

"We did the mambo offense," said Friedgen. "One, two, three, punt."

Clemson ground out another long drive that led to another field goal. A Jones pass was deflected off a tall defensive lineman and intercepted. Another drive, another field goal. Some more mambo.

"We should have continued to play it loose," said Ross. "That's the only way you can deal with a defense like that. They were a dominating defense. If you'll remember in the Citrus Bowl, we continued to play loose. I was bound and determined I was never gonna let that happen again, particularly when you're going up against a team of that magnitude, where you know they've got some dominating people. Nebraska was the same way. I remember Ralph said, 'You wanna keep it on the ground?' I said, 'Keep it loose.' We were throwing the ball till the end. I learned from the Clemson game, big time."

"When the coaches got conservative, we were very upset about that," said Tom Covington. "When we were up 14–0, we said, 'OK, let's air it out.' They said, 'OK, let's develop the running game.'

"Watching the defense in the third quarter was very frustrating. I think that carried over to our play. We wanted to make something happen so bad. We also felt pressure that we can't let this slip away. The defense was getting tired and we had to make a play. You're a team, but you know if you're the defense, you're ticked off because you were just out there for nine minutes and you've gotta go out there again."

And again. And again. "We always said during practice, 'Man, we'll never get in a game that's as hard as practice, we're doing

Coleman Rudolph celebrates his fumble recovery against Clemson.

all this constant running,' " said Kevin Battle. "Well, no one said that after the Clemson game. The third and fourth quarters were the most exhausting of any game I've ever had. We stayed out there so looooong."

For 13 minutes in the third quarter, another 12 in the fourth. In the entire second half, Tech ran just 11 offensive plays. The Jackets' defense was exhausted. A couple of times, defenders went down and intentionally stayed down, hoping to gain a few precious seconds of rest. "One time," said Marco Coleman, "Calvin made a tackle and laid down. He faked it. That helped a

Kevin Tisdel returns kickoff 87 yards versus Clemson . . .

lot. In the third quarter, I couldn't breathe.''

"In the last quarter," said Jerimiah McClary, "I was just going on instinct and emotion. I know a lot of guys looked up to me. If I showed I was tired and slacked off, they'd follow my cue. I couldn't let them down. So, 'Put the ball down, ref.' Our attitude was, that's what we're on scholarship to do: play defense.

"But it was just a slugfest out there. Once they lined up with two tight ends, they started playing smashmouth and we had to do the same thing. With the defense, it began to be a game within a game, to see who could make the next big play."

Or who could hear the defensive signals. The game was so intense, the crowd so vocal, "We had to scream in the huddle to call signals," said Balkcom.

"That's 19!" the south scoreboard proclaimed at the end of the third quarter. For Tech's defense, the season-long, no-TD

string had reached 19 quarters. Just 12 seconds into the fourth, though, Clemson's Chris Gardocki kicked his fourth field goal to cut it to 14–12. And then it was Tisdel time.

Earlier that week, Kevin Tisdel had asked Ross for a chance to return kickoffs. Ross agreed and the sophomore walk-on lined up deep. His presence was even more critical once Swilling was injured, but never more than now, when it was 14–12 and when Tisdel embodied his nickname: "Cut It Up," for his slashing, open-field moves.

Fielding the kickoff in the end zone, Tisdel started up the left side, then made a slashing, diagonal move near midfield to avoid the lunging Gardocki. He crossed left-to-right to a mighty roar, racing 87 yards before he was finally downed at the Clemson 13. Two plays later, Tech faced a third-and-3 at the 6, and Ralph Friedgen faced a big decision. Timeout, Tech.

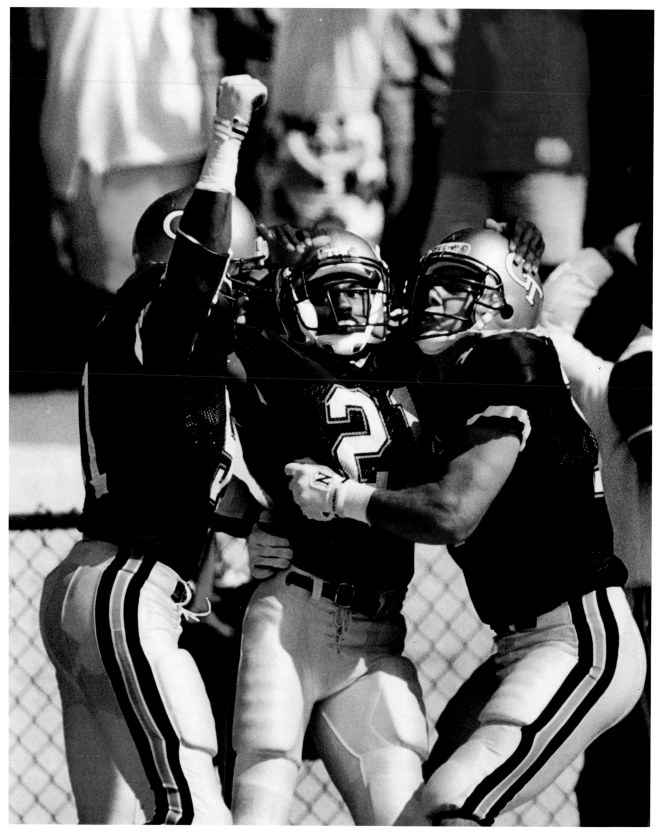

. . . then celebrates with teammates.

JACK WILKINSON

On the phones, Friedgen told Ross he wanted to call a pass play. Ross demurred. So Friedgen suggested a staple of Tech's offense: 45 slant, the tailback following full-back Stefen Scotton's lead block.

"You want to run it now?" Ross asked.

"Let's run it," said Friedgen. "They'll be thinking pass."

Friedgen was merely hoping to make a first down. He called 45 slant, aligned Tech in a three-wideout formation and told Shawn Jones to check the play at the line, audible if necessary. Jones didn't. Clemson blitzed and Jones ran the play smack into the blitz. But something remarkable happened, as it would all season for Tech.

"The two guys [blitzers] came off on Shawn on the [bootleg] fake," said Friedgen. "Stefen chopped the linebacker and T.J. Edwards split them and scored. Why I changed, I don't know. I'm not normally like that. It was, like, five or six plays in the season a play came in my mind and I did it. It probably didn't make any sense to do it, but it worked. Some divine guidance was working. I was saying, 'I can't believe it.' Then I saw what they ran into: we ran into a play that should be dead, but two guys came off on Shawn and Stefen had a great block and so did Lavin and Jenkins, and T.J. just walked in.

"That was a big touchdown. If we had kicked a field goal there, we would have lost the game. We won that game because we scored touchdowns and they kicked field goals."

Clemson did score one touchdown. But not before yet another remarkable defensive stand by Georgia Tech. Clemson responded to Edwards's TD by grinding 78 yards to the Tech 1. The Tech coaching staff had told the defense that Clemson would probably score, but not to dwell on it or let it alter the defensive assignments. Now the Tigers were telling Tech precisely the same thing.

As Clemson mounted its drive, the offensive line broke the huddle and came to the line shouting, "We're gonna score! We're gonna get in!" This amused, more than infuriated, the Jackets.

"Here's high-powered, ranked Clemson, they're not yelling, 'We're gonna beat you!'" said McClary. "They were just concerned about scoring."

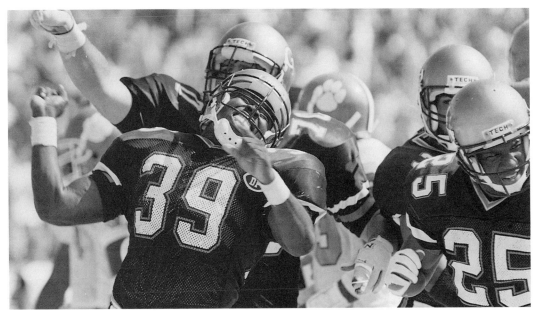

T. J. Edwards comes off the field celebrating after his fourth-quarter score.

Tech was just as adamant with stopping them. On fourth and 1, Tech was in its goal-line defense, a 92 scheme (nine men on the line, two backers) with a gap call. Defensive linemen were supposed to fill the gap. When the Clemson center tried to cut Kevin Battle, the noseguard blasted the right guard. "And there he was," said Battle. There was fullback Derrick Witherspoon coming at him, carrying the ball. And here came Calvin Tiggle, freed up to make the hit when McClary occupied the offensive tackle.

"This might sound funny, but everything seemed to be going in slow motion," said Battle. "Witherspoon was fast, but slow. I saw him running, it felt like I could hear him breathing. I even saw his eyes get real big and I thought, 'He's getting ready to do something.' I just reached out, and grabbed him."

So did Tiggle, who dived and hit Witherspoon head-first. Together, they downed him at the 1. Tech ball, and with 8:04 left, Tech still led 21–12. The defense, and stadium, went berserk. For good measure, Battle reached down, put his hand on Witherspoon's helmet and announced, "You're not getting in there! Don't think you're ever getting in there!"

Naturally, less than five minutes later, Clemson got in there.

Tech ground out a couple of first downs, but then Edwards fumbled and Clemson recovered at the Jackets' 41. When Cameron scored on a 3-yard keeper, Clemson rejoiced. Someone had finally scored on Tech's defense, Clemson trailed by just 21–19 and there was still 3:27 remaining. And Gardocki's foot was in fine form.

"That's when the fear set," said Battle. "When you have a kicker like Gardocki . . . , well, I played him in the Georgia [high school] all-star game. One time, the ball was on the 50 and he kicked it and it fell

short. The players who knew him said, 'Would you quit playing around and please kick it through the goal post?!' He lined it up again and BOOM! It went through."

Gardocki got another chance. Tech managed one first down, but then a third-down swing pass to Scotton, wide open in the right flat, was dropped. Tech had to punt— and Scott Aldredge promptly shanked it. The ball went straight up, then landed and started bouncing backward. It was downed at the Tech 49, just an 11-yard punt—but it could have been worse. For it was Aldredge who downed the punt. As distraught as he was, had Aldredge not hustled and downed the ball, it might have bounced further into Tech territory—and further into Gardocki's range.

"At this point, we were playing and praying at the same time," McClary said. "We knew one big play and Gardocki would be in range."

Indeed, Gardocki had once kicked a 57-yard field goal. This time, he would be called on for a 60-yarder. Three plays— including a pass call that fell incomplete— generated six yards. Before the third-down play, McClary and Coleman glanced at each other.

"Marco and I had been in the game forever, it seemed," said McClary. "We'd played every snap. He looked at me and shook his head and I looked at him and we both started laughing. I'm not sure if we were delirious, or what."

Delirium followed shortly. On the Tech sidelines, some coaches and players looked, some couldn't bear to. All prayed, many clasping bowing heads and clasping each other's hands. "The only time I would have doubts about him," Battle said of Gardocki, "is if it were a 99-yarder."

On the field, the defense made a block call. Willie Clay came flying, then diving in from the right. His outstretched arms and

Chris Gardocki's last-minute field goal falls short for Clemson.

After win over Clemson, players join students in traditional "Ramblin' Wreck" fight song.

JACK WILKINSON

hands missed the ball. Not to worry. Gardocki missed, too.

His field goal attempt fell short. "AWESOME!" read the scoreboard. Tech ran out the final 59 seconds, then ran amok. "The fat lady sings," flashed the scoreboard, then: "Good Guys 21 Bad Guys 19." Battle, who had been kneeling on the sideline in silent prayer, leaped in the air, then lumbered onto the field, dancing and gyrating with Calvin Tiggle before embracing him.

"That's a victory dance," Battle said. More like an act of attrition. Clemson had controlled the ball for an astounding 25 minutes and 7 seconds in the second half. And yet, Tech still won. Spying O'Leary on the field, Battle said, "Coach, you put the ball down a lot this game!"

"Yeah," said O'Leary, "you got a chance to get better, didn't you?" Indeed, Tech's defense was on the field for 98 plays. A doubleheader.

Upstairs in the press box, Ralph Friedgen stood and marveled at the sight below him. The entire stadium was standing, the ovation pouring down on the Jackets. Friedgen reflected on that awful day at Wake Forest in '87, then absorbed the scene before him. He had never seen such emotion at Tech, not even after the victory over Georgia the previous year. Then Friedgen turned to John Misciagna, Tech's director of recruiting, and said, "Boy, there's nothing like this."

As always after a victory, the Jackets assembled in front of the student section in the East Stands and sang "The Rambling Wreck" fight song. Inside the locker room, the Jackets exulted.

"A war," Marlon Williams called the game. "An all-out battle. We played with square helmets today. That's how much we hit."

In the interview room, Tisdel responded to his first flirtation with the media with aplomb. "I don't just want to be in the press guide next year," he said. "I want to be on the cover."

And Ross reveled in his most significant victory at Tech. "As gutty a performance as I've ever been around," he said. "We were just hanging on, we were so tired. They were just pounding us to death and there wasn't a lot we could do. We just knocked the hell out of each other. They probably knocked the hell out of us more than we did them. But we found a way to win."

And never mind those who wondered whether Tech truly deserved to win. "You're damn right, 'cause we found a way to win," said Ross. "It wasn't pretty but when you go against a great football team, it's not gonna be pretty. And I thought they were the best team we played all year."

The hallway outside the Tech locker room was jammed. Among them was Jack Rudolph, who played during the Dodd days and whose son is Coleman Rudolph. "I remember three, four years ago," Rudolph said, "you could walk in here and nobody was around."

Outside the Edge Center, a kid was selling $2 placards, which were printed up immediately after the game. They bore the final score and more: "How 'Bout Them Yellow Jackets! 5 and Oh!"

"We didn't back down at all," said Clay. "That was the thing I was worried about. You know, some people talk a lot but they get scared at the initial punch. But everybody stood their ground and took the blows. It was like a big heavyweight fight, it just kept going back and forth. And we survived."

"Once we beat Clemson," said Shawn Jones, "everybody felt we beat the best team in the conference."

Everybody felt something else, too: Tired.

"After that game, nobody went out," said

Marco Coleman. "Too tired. I just went back to the room and had a couple of beers. I was so exhausted, I didn't have anything left. The only thing I could do was open up my mouth for beers. Had to have a straw for that. My arms were too tired to pick up the can."

With the feeling of exhaustion, though, came a feeling of invincibility. "After that game, we felt nobody could beat us," Coleman said. "Standing up to that team on the goal line like we did, we felt nobody could beat us."

Beat up, though? Most definitely. When the Jackets reassembled the next day, the locker room was a grim reminder. "Like a war zone," Ross recalled.

Swilling was already on crutches and in agony, his ankle swollen to humongous proportions. He feared it was chipped. Not so; but Swilling would miss the next two games. Even the healthy players were dragging. How draining had the Clemson game been? As usual, Kevin Battle weighed in after the Clemson game; he weighed in again when the Jackets reported back on Sunday. In less than 24 hours, he'd gained 18 pounds. "What did you eat?" O'Leary asked him. "Your dog?"

"Just a sub and a few sodas," claimed Battle. Which sub? The Nautilus?

Mike Mooney had been admitted to Piedmont Hospital on Saturday. In the South Carolina game, Mark Hutto had accidentally stepped on Mooney's hand while both were pulling and blocking on Stefen Scotton's TD sweep. Mooney's hand bled through the tape and black gloves he wore. His left finger was badly swollen, black and blue. He taped it up and finished that game, then took medication to play against Maryland. The fingernail was coming off; after the Clemson game, doctors feared the entire finger might have to come off, the infection so bad that amputation seemed a distinct possibility. The finger was surgically opened and cleaned, and tests were performed. Mooney was hospitalized a couple of days and was finally released on Thursday. He would not play at North Carolina.

"If we lose because something stupid happens," Mooney told his mother after the Clemson game, "I'll just be furious."

"If I had to do it all over," Mooney says now, "I'd have played the North Carolina game."

chapter

By now, the Jackets were on the cusp of the Top 10, ranked 11th and rising rapidly. And for the first time, Virginia was ranked No. 1, setting the stage for Charlottesville two weeks hence. At the moment, though, Georgia Tech had far greater concerns: the loss of Ken Swilling and Mike Mooney.

Swilling dreams, often. Two weeks prior, he'd dreamt about being on crutches.

"I didn't know what that meant," Swilling said. "I was just dreaming I was on crutches and going down a hallway and I was very frustrated. A lot of times, I forget my dreams and then when I have them it's like deja vu."

So was this one. The deja view, though, was awful. In the dream, Swilling took a crutch and slammed it against the wall, so frustrated was he at being on crutches. "I didn't actually remember that," he said, "until I hit the wall with the crutch."

Sure enough, a couple of days before the Carolina game, Swilling was walking down the hallway in his dormitory when he took his crutch and took out his frustrations by slamming the crutch into the wall. "I was just so frustrated, I wanted to be out there and help my team," he said. "As soon as I did that, it was, 'Wait a minute. I've been here before.' "

If that premonition was painful, Saturday afternoon was absolutely nightmarish for Tech. Chapel Hill became Chapel Hell for the Jackets, especially Swilling, Mooney and Willie Clay.

Mooney didn't make the trip, staying home in Atlanta and staying tuned to the game on radio. Without him, and with an early injury to Russell Freeman compounding the offensive line's problems, Mooney's mates up front endured a long, frustrating day. "I felt terrible," Mooney said. "I felt like I let those guys down. Four seniors there, and they'd been through hell. I could have played some. I could at least have given those guys a break."

Tom Covington plays catch-and-run against North Carolina.

Perhaps. Swilling, though, could not have. He hitched a ride to Chapel Hill with linebacker Scott Travis and his brother, and spent the afternoon on the sideline, but not on crutches. To his regret.

"It was something I probably shouldn't have done," said Swilling. "It hurt so bad; I didn't know how to feel, standing on the sideline and not being able to help my teammates. It just felt so awkward to be there and not be able to play. I felt really helpless."

Almost as helpless as Tech's offensive felt on every venture near the goal line. Elsewhere, the Jackets were nearly flawless, ringing up 435 yards total offense to just 151 for Carolina. The Jackets sputtered and gasped in their goal line offense, though,

JACK WILKINSON

Shawn Jones scored Tech's lone TD against the 'Heels.

and a costly turnover by Clay led to Carolina's lone touchdown.

Even before the game began, though, several Tech coaches and players sensed trouble. Twice that week, Ross called team meetings and stressed that the Jackets could not become complacent. After arriving in Chapel Hill on Friday, Joe Siffri and Darryl Jenkins called a similar meeting of the offensive line. Then there was the arrival in Chapel Hill itself.

"I think it all started when we got off the bus there," said Balkcom. "They had some very beautiful young ladies meet us and they gave us candy and all this kind of stuff. Right when we went to practice Friday. Welcome to Chapel Hill. I think that really threw everybody on their heels. We started to relax."

It was mid-term week at Tech. On Friday, Ralph Friedgen went recruiting in Georgia, then flew to North Carolina early that evening. When he and O'Leary returned to the hotel after dinner to do some more game preparation, Friedgen noticed several players hanging out in the lobby and hallways, some talking on the phone to girls. It was all so out of character for the Jackets and it concerned Friedgen.

On Saturday, when the Jackets took the field for pre-game warmups, Joe Siffri turned to Dr. Blane Woodfin, Tech's orthopedic consultant, and said, "Something doesn't feel right. I really don't have a good feeling about this game."

"At that point," Siffri recalled, "we were so confident in our ability, we started to get big-headed, which hadn't gotten us to where we were."

Being big-headed and short-handed on the offensive line was Tech's undoing. Carolina capitalized on Bell's fumble at the Tech 29 for an early 3–0 lead. Jones scored on a risky, third-and-1, 26-yard bootleg in the second quarter; then Scott Sisson kicked a field goal after the Jackets stalled at the Tar Heel 3 for a 10–3 halftime lead.

"But it was the same old story," said Tom Covington. "North Carolina has played us tough ever since I've been here, whether they're 1–10 or 11–0. I don't know, maybe they have our playbooks. But a couple of people admitted they overlooked them and didn't put their total efforts in them. And it cost us. That was very distasteful."

Another turnover, this time a Jones interception, led to another Carolina field goal late in the third quarter. Early in the fourth, Clay muffed a punt and the Heels recovered at the Tech 7. Two plays later, Natrone Means' 5-yard TD put Carolina up 13–10.

On its next possession, Tech drove 85 yards, riding Bell toward a touchdown. After an incompletion on first-and-goal at the 4, Bell burst three yards up the middle to the 1. Then Tech's shortcoming's on the offensive line were exposed. In Tech's goal-line offense, the line is usually Lavin and Mark Hutto at the guards, Veryl Miller at center, Mooney and Russell Freeman the tackles. But Mooney hadn't even made the trip and Freeman broke his wrist early in the game. So Tech had to go with Jenkins (hampered by a painful left shoulder bruise) at left tackle, Hutto (nursing a bad elbow) at left guard, Miller at center, Siffri at right guard and the undersized Lavin, using a left-handed stance, at right tackle. "It was obvious we missed Mike and Russell," said Lavin.

It was never more obvious than in the fourth quarter. On third down, Bell was stopped for no gain. Ross disdained a field goal, figuring that if North Carolina stopped Tech, his defense would hold the Heels, force a punt and Tech would have good field position. On fourth down, Ross ran Stefen Scotton off the right side. It became the wrong side.

"I didn't get a very good block," said Lavin. "Me and the tight end [Covington] didn't do a real good job." Eric Gash did, the blitzing Carolina linebacker meeting Scotton head-on and stopping him for no gain. It was the second time that day that Tech had driven inside the opposition's 5-yard line and failed to score. Those were the only times that would happen all season.

As Ross had hoped, Carolina was forced to punt and Jones promptly hit Covington for 38 yards to the Heels' 8. When the Jackets again stalled, though, Sisson came on to kick a tying, 27-yard field goal with 61 seconds left. Initially, many of the Jackets were upset that Ross went for the field goal. "I was angry," Battle said. "I felt like we shouldn't tie UNC."

Lavin was distraught, weeping in the locker room and telling himself, "I can't believe we lost that football game."

"To me," he said later, "it was a loss."

To Ross, it most assuredly wasn't. It was a tie, and the critics be damned. "We still kept things within our own control," said Ross. "If we lose the game, we've gotta rely on somebody else to win the conference. If we tie, then we still play everybody. And if we win, everybody else has a loss and we win the conference."

There would be even farther-reaching consequences. Had Tech gone for the touchdown against Carolina, and missed, thus ending the season at 11–1 instead of 11–0–1, "We probably don't end up in the top 5," said Ross.

"I felt we had dodged a bullet," said Ross. "I wasn't down at all. You didn't like that blemish, but everything was still there for us. Nothing had been removed."

But something had been restored: Tech's sense of self. Its true self.

"That game really woke us up," said Jones. "We felt like we could go undefeated but felt like we couldn't get beat. After that game, we went back to basics, the little things."

"It taught us we were still Georgia Tech," said Siffri. "We've still gotta play our best game in order to compete. That got us back on track and made us doubt ourselves just enough to get us going again."

"A wakening call," Covington called it. "We had so many people on Cloud 9. It brought us back down to earth. Remember how we got here: hard work. Can't let up. And any time we're in a position to score, we must score."

All of this pleased the coaching staff immensely. "At that point, I didn't know where we were," said Friedgen. "Coach was very calm, though, and told the team after the game, 'You didn't play well, I'm very

disappointed but it could be a lot worse. The world's not over. We're still in this thing.'

"The kids . . . I was interested to hear some of the comments. They took it like a loss. That made me feel a little bit better, to be honest. There were times when we would be happy to have a tie. So it kinda tells me where they're coming from. You have to understand, some of our kids here had never really ever been patted on the back, and told that they were good. Even last year, it was kinda like they've always been put down, everything they read, everything they hear on campus. North Carolina was a learning experience and something they had to work their way through."

The low point of the year: a 13–13 tie with North Carolina.

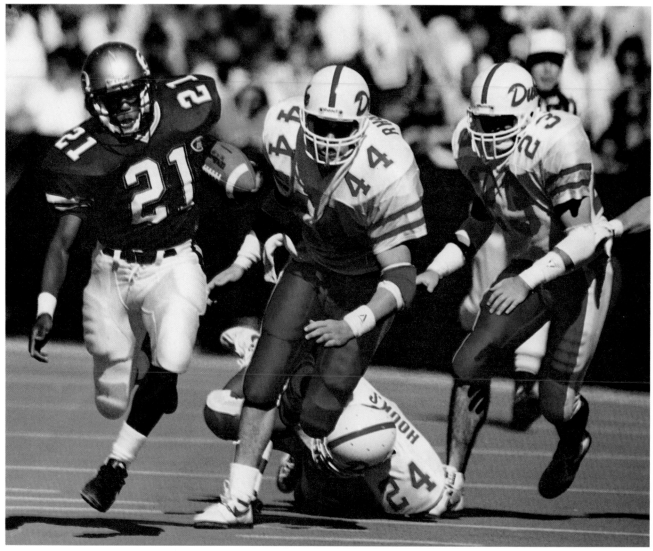

Tisdel returns kickoff for a TD versus Duke . . .

chapter

And you thought Duke basketball fans were obnoxious?

"Duke's one of the most talkative teams," said Mike Mooney. "They talk a lot of trash."

As if the Halloween '87 scoreboard memory ("Welcome to the Basement, Tekkies") weren't enough. As if former Duke coach Steve Spurrier's vow never to lose to Georgia Tech weren't enough. As if three straight losses to Duke weren't enough. As if Spurrier calling for a sixth TD pass in the waning minutes in '87 weren't enough. For all those reasons, and to soothe their eardrums, the Jackets wanted Duke badly.

And that's nearly how they got Duke.

By now, the ACC and national possibilities were tantalizing. Even Ralph Friedgen couldn't restrain himself. He told George O'Leary, "We could win this whole thing."

"What?!" answered O'Leary.

"If we beat Duke and beat Virginia,"

Friedgen said, "we got a chance."

"George just kinda shook it off: 'Yeah, yeah, yeah, we'll see,'" said Friedgen. But such thinking was prevalent on The Flats, and continued on up to Virginia. For that, Georgia Tech can thank Kevin Tisdel.

The dress list—those players who will dress out in uniform for Saturday's game—is posted each Thursday at Tech. On the Thursday before the homecoming game against Duke, a dejected and distraught Tisdel talked with Kevin Battle in the locker room. Inexplicably, Tisdel had been left off the dress list for Duke.

"He was really hurt about that, really upset," Battle said. "I told him the best thing to do is go up and talk to Coach Ross. Don't talk to other people, the players, any coaches, go to the big man. Just ask him. And if he says he left you off, then just go out there and do your thing again, and see what happens next week."

Tisdel balked. He'd waited long enough,

and accomplished enough, to warrant dressing out, if not a scholarship. Tisdel was so upset, he'd already called his family back home in Columbus and announced his intention to quit. Battle dissuaded him and convinced him to see Ross.

When Ross spied Tisdel, he noticed the long face immediately. When Tisdel explained, the coach was as perplexed as the player was upset. In truth, Tisdel had inadvertently been left off the dress list. Somehow, Ross had pulled out an old dress list, one that didn't include Tisdel. Ross reassured Tisdel that he was not only dressing out but returning kickoffs. It was one of his best, if easiest, coaching decisions of the season.

When Tisdel returned to the locker room, Kevin Battle was stepping out of the shower. He noticed the huge smile on Tisdel's face. The players laughed and joked about it. Battle was genuinely thrilled for his friend. Two days later, he was eternally grateful.

Determined to dominate on homecoming, Tech promptly drove to a touchdown on its first possession. William Bell, who would rush for 166 yards, scored from four yards out for a 7–0 lead that Tech would never relinquish. But not before some sky-high anxiety.

Late in the third quarter, a Billy Ray-to-Randy Cuthbert pass trimmed Tech's lead to 24–21. The Blue Devils seemed on the verge of doing it, again.

Duke perenially gives Tech problems with its passing game. The Blue Devils isolate their receivers one on one; if defenders miss tackles, an afternoon can seem interminable. Against Duke, Tech played a lot of nickel coverage (five defensive backs) and conceded the short, five-yard pass in certain coverages. But the Jackets' tackling was sloppy that day, their pursuit poor, and Billy Ray and his receivers were toying with

Tech. The Jackets' best defensive play of the day came immediately after Ray leveled Coleman with a crack-back block on a reverse. On the next play, Chris Simmons blindsided Ray and sent his helmet flying 10 yards in the air.

"We'd hit a kid and I didn't see anyone coming in for the second hit," O'Leary said. "That's the first game where I was disappointed leaving the field. I didn't see that great intensity we should see in our people, because we're a blue-collar team. We don't have any great players. I mean, there are no great players out there, there really aren't. I don't care who the free safety [Swilling] is, there's no great players. We've got good players and they've got to play at their top level for us to win."

Now leading by just 24–21 with more than 17 minutes to play, Tech was in trouble. And then Tisdel reaffirmed Ross's faith in him.

Reaffirmation lasted 85 yards and 15 seconds. That's how long it took Tisdel to take back the kickoff for the decisive touchdown. It was an astonishing effort. Tisdel was hit by seven different defenders. He somehow shook them all off and scored, providing Tech a 10-point cushion en route to a 48–31 win.

"Offensively, that was the game where we started to jell, started to take off," said Ross. "And it came at a perfect time. Our defense was starting to wear down. Our offense needed to take some pressure off the defense."

"Offensively, we did it all," said Shawn Jones, who scored twice and gained 77 of Tech's 316 yards rushing. "We ran the ball well, ran power plays well, short yardage plays well, ran the passing game well, maintained ball control. We did it all that game. We were peaking."

And so was Kevin Tisdel. Willie Clay offered to call Tisdel "The Rocket," as in

Rocket Ismail. Or even "The Bomb." "I don't care," Clay said, "just as long as he keeps exploding."

Bobby Ross called Tisdel something even more meaningful: a scholarship player. "Now, before I get asked the question, Kevin Tisdel now has a scholarship," Ross said in his post-game press conference. "I told him after the game that I'm not holding it any longer. He'll have that scholarship. That son of a gun gets it going for us. This is the second ballgame in which his big play had something to do with winning the football game."

Battle, for one, was thrilled for Tisdel. "I was so happy for him," Battle said.

"Kevin has a strong belief in God and I think that's what helped him get his scholarship. I'm a real strong believer in things happen for particular reasons. I really believe that was a blessing he had for being so patient. Every practice, he's out there doing the drills diligently. He's not complaining about it. I just think there's a blessing for that. I told him, 'Thank God it was right.' I mean, that's something that everyone wants, a free ride through school."

"Now that I've got that scholarship, I've got to get myself a new goal," Tisdel said after the game, and after Ross's announcement. "Right now, I just want to help us keep winning games."

. . . then gets mobbed on the sidelines.

Ross gets a Gatorade bath.

chapter

Memorable moments abound in Georgia Tech history, football games of surpassing significance and legend. The 222–0 Cumberland game. Roy Riegels' wrong-way Rose Bowl run. The Baylor-Pepper Rodgers field goal Orange Bowl. The perfection that was '52. Jakie Rudolph knocking Alabama, and himself, unconscious in '52. The 7–6 upset of No. 1 'Bama and The Bear in '62. And yet the perhaps greatest game in Tech history took place on a breathtakingly beautiful autumn afternoon on the grounds of Mr. Jefferson's university, with a capacity crowd enthralled, as well as a national television audience and a killer whale circling high overhead. What a threesome they proved to be: Thomas Jefferson, Scott Sisson and Shamu.

"The Brawl For It All," a Virginia paper called it. And no one flinched, everyone buying the hype. And why not? This was No. 16 Georgia Tech versus Virginia. Top-ranked, undefeated, 7-and-oh-can-they-score Virginia. With Shawn Moore passing to Herman Moore, the Cavaliers rang up points faster than a cashier rings up the grocery register on double-coupon days. They led the nation in scoring (48.1 points per game) and total offense (544.9 yards) and Moore was the country's No. 1-rated passer.

The showdown's significance was undeniable. At stake: two unbeaten records, one spotless. The ACC championship. And the national championship. It transcended the first week of November and became the college football game of the season. And the ticket of the season.

How great was the demand? Tech received just 1,000 tickets to Scott Stadium. Ten times that might not have sufficed; 10,000 might have traveled the 517 miles from Atlanta to Charlottesville. The frenzy on The Flats was out of control. And Marco

Coleman tried to control himself.

"Playing the No. 1 team in the country, on CBS, is what I'd been looking forward to all my life—except for going to the pros," said Coleman. "I was so excited, I didn't know what to do."

"Virginia was like one of those games when I was growing up," said Willie Clay. "We used to watch CBS and used to watch games, and it would come down to the end. And it was, like, 'Gee, I would love to play in a game like that.' I couldn't wait to play in that type of environment, when people are screaming at you. I always dreamed of it."

Bobby Ross was even more excited than his players. But then, he always gets like that for games like this. "He lives for the big games," said Bryant. "He loves coaching against Penn State. He thrives on coaching at Clemson." Yet this was one big game that, for Ross, grew exponentially enormous.

"I was probably as emotional for that football game as I'd been all year long," said Ross. "I was ready to play that game Monday. I had to really control my emotions. I didn't want us to get ready too early."

There were all the obvious elements: No. 1. Network TV. An opponent whom Ross had never beaten at Tech and one he'd played against in college. An opponent that was the state university in his native state. And an elderly father coming over from Williamsburg to see his son's team. "And," said Ross, "I don't know if it's gonna be the last game he'd get to see."

Bus Ross, age 86, had undergone sextuple bypass surgery the previous April, yet felt strong enough to travel to Charlottesville for the most important game in his son's coaching career. But then, his father wasn't the only relative whose presence Ross felt.

On Friday evening, Ross got a telephone call at the team hotel. It was his son Chris calling from a pay phone in Big Springs, Texas. Chris and his wife, Deann, had driven nine hours from their home in New Mexico to San Antonio, where Deann underwent a sonogram. She was pregnant again. This time, the entire Ross family prayed everything was all right with the baby.

Chris and Deann's first child, Rebecca, was born with a congenital heart defect. She was a lovely little girl who, despite her health problems, delighted and lifted all those around her, especially her paternal grandfather. Bobby Ross was heartbroken when Rebecca, just 15 months old, died in March of 1990. He insisted that the complete Ross family portrait—the one with Rebecca sitting on his lap— be printed in the Tech media guide.

Now Deann was pregnant again. And the family was worried, again. "The doctors had said you had a higher risk of that type of thing [heart abnormality] happening again after it's happened," said Ross. But at 9 o'clock on the night before the Virginia game, Bobby Ross got the phone call he'd been hoping for. It was freezing and snowing in Big Springs, with the wind whipping through the chilled night air, when Chris Ross said, "Daddy, everything's all right. The sonogram shows everything is perfect. Looks like we got a little boy."

"That lifted me 20 feet off the ground," said Ross, beaming at the memory. "I was so excited. It was like [he rubbed his hands together], 'Now let's go play.' It wasn't that it was gonna be a distraction for me in the game. But it took a burden off me and my wife, too."

If Ross was ready to play, so were his players. As if the game itself, and its conference and national implications, weren't incentive enough, the Jackets had arrived in Charlottesville carrying all kinds of

The Ross clan at home.

slights, real and imagined. Even now, some Jackets find it hard to bring up the putdowns.

"I'm trying to get my thoughts together," Kevin Battle began hesitantly. "My true feelings about it are so full. It wasn't just a game; it was a personal vendetta. Extremely personal. Those people criticized us, and I don't know why. I don't know why they said the things they said, did some of the things they did, as far as the news media is concerned. For the whole team, this became not just a game but a war. What they said about Swilling during the week, and the defensive line, that was uncalled for. They had their offensive tackle saying he was just going to destroy Jerimiah. Then, of course, what they said

about how we're not worthy to play with them. Even flying up to Virginia, I saw little signs that said, 'Virginia, ACC Championship, No. 1 in the Nation,' before they even played us."

"They were extremely arrogant," said McClary. "They were mocking us and said we'd played soft teams—the same teams they'd played. And all the stuff they put in the paper about us and making fun of Ken."

Virginia—specifically defensive back Tony Covington—had been highly critical of Ken Swilling. Covington felt that Swilling, even before his injury, was overrated and couldn't contain Herman Moore, UVA's gifted, 6–5 All-America wideout. During the season, the Tech sports information office produced a promotional poster of Swilling (who had switched his jersey number to No. 1 for 1990), calling him, "A Force of One." Now he was being lampooned as "A Farce of One."

Charlottesville, usually so staid and oh-so-preppy, was absolutely aglow, basking in anticipation of the biggest football game in UVA history. The Cavaliers' confidence was infectious, and why not? They'd opened the season with their first-ever victory over Clemson and had annihilated the next six opponents, including a 59–0 thrashing of Duke. All season, the main thoroughfare through town had been adorned with giant orange Vs, painted before the opener, to simulate the orange tiger paws paving the way to Clemson's Death Valley. This would also be homecoming at UVA, as well as a Friday night intrasquad basketball game featuring celebrity guest coaches Woody Harrelson and Bruce Hornsby.

Mr. Jefferson's school had never seen such giddiness over football. And then there was Shamu: all week, the blimp from Orlando's Sea World, as part of the game's Citrus Bowl pomp, hovered above Charlottesville. Painted like Shamu, a killer whale and Sea World's major attraction, the blimp was a constant reminder in the sky of Saturday's showdown.

Virginia, though, oozed confidence. Surprisingly, and privately, so did Tech. Especially Ralph Friedgen. That Wednesday, Friedgen took a call from Tim Brant, the CBS play-by-play announcer who played for Friedgen at Maryland.

Brant: "Tell me something that's gonna make me look smart."

Friedgen: "I'll only tell you something that makes you look smart if you make me look smart."

Brant: "It's a deal."

Friedgen: "We're gonna win. I'm giving you the first news tip."

Friedgen still laughs about that. "He said, 'Ah, come on, Ralph. They got Shawn Moore and that high-powered offense.' I said, 'We got a pretty good defense.' He said, 'They got a pretty good defense, too.' I said, 'Yeah, they are. But we got a pretty good offense. I think we match up pretty well.'"

Long after the game, and after watching a tape of it and hearing Brant's comments that seemed so pro-Virginia, Friedgen wrote him a note: "Timmy, I tried to teach you sports, but you're still dumb as hell."

Saturday morning broke crisp and clear and gorgeous. It also broke damn early for Bobby Ross. At 6 a.m., he got a phone call from Homer Rice. In the middle of the night, vandals had broken into Scott Stadium and set a portion of the artificial turf on fire. Initially, the damage was feared to be so extensive that Rice told Ross, "We may not play this game."

Ross and Virginia coach George Welsh met their athletic directors at the stadium. A patch of turf had indeed been burned, but after conferring with his maintenance crew, UVA AD Jim Copeland was confident the field could be repaired with leftover artificial turf from the Virginia baseball diamond. This scorched earth policy wouldn't impede anyone. Upon examination, both coaches gave the field their blessings. Then they, and their teams, blessed college football with an afternoon of greatness.

When the Jackets arrived at Scott Stadium Saturday morning, even two hours before kickoff, the parking fields were full, fans were everywhere and Virginia students had stormed the gate leading to the student section, desperate to get decent seats on the grassy, curved hillside of the horseshoe. Upon dressing, the Jackets ambled out into the stadium for a pre-game warmup more enervating than most games themselves.

This was a Virginia crowd? "The fans

Offensive coordinator Ralph Friedgen on the phone.

Shawn Moore meets Marco Coleman.

were spitting at you," said William Bell, "throwing ice and soda cups at you, calling you names. It was just great, the stuff that college football was actually made out of. It gets you kind of hyped up, because that's what you dream about when you think about college football: playing in front of big crowds, on television. And not just cable TV, I'm talking worldwide TV. When the people without cable can see you without a satellite dish, that's saying a lot.

"That's when I knew that Tech was getting some kind of notoriety. Fans just don't hate you because you're not a good team. They hate you because you're going to cause problems with their team."

Perceptive people, William Bell and those Wahoo fans. But at the outset, an upset seemed unlikely. No, laughably absurd.

"Virginia just came out winging," said Ross. "We said if we can just take the big play out of it, we'll be OK. And that was all they were doing."

On the game's second play, Shawn Moore evaded a blitz, and the Virginia quarterback hit a bomb to Herman Moore. It was the first of Herman Moore's nine receptions that day, for an astounding 234 yards, and it led to Shawn Moore's 1-yard TD and a 7–0 lead. When Jake McInerney kicked his second field goal just 10 seconds into the second quarter, Virginia led 13–0 and Tech dreaded what the next 45 minutes might hold.

"We really thought we were gonna beat 'em pretty bad," recalled Mooney. At 13–0, though, as the offensive line sat on the Tech bench, the linemen stared at each other in disbelief. When Tech took over, as Mooney and Darryl Jenkins walked onto the field, Jenkins turned to Mooney and warned, "If we don't score this time, Mike, the game is gonna be over. They're gonna score, they're gonna score."

"You could see it," Mooney said. "They were gonna outscore us."

Shawn Jones would not let that happen. He drove the Jackets 75 yards, scrambling the last 23 yards himself to trim it to 13–7. On the sidelines, the Tech offense soared with confidence, certain of its ability to score from anywhere, any time. "The way Shawn was throwing and playing, if the offensive line gave Shawn any time at all, something good was gonna happen," Mooney said. "There was a feeling in the huddle after that like, 'Just get us back to the line. As soon as we get back there, something else good is gonna happen.' We were coming out of the huddle real fast, weren't using much of the 30-second clock. I think we were tiring 'em out, wearing 'em down."

Perhaps, but not until the second half. By then, Tech had overcome — sort of — another obstacle: the phones.

"As frustrating as all git-out," said Ross. "Only the offensive phones were messed up, not the defense. But there never was a time in the whole game where it was totally running smoothly. We kept switching the phones from offense to defense. I don't know if somebody was playing with 'em or not."

From the opening kickoff, Friedgen had problems with the phone upstairs in the coaches' booth that was his lifeline to the sideline and Ross. The lifeline kept going dead, again and again and again. "Coach Ross gets excited like any head coach," Friedgen said. "I could hear him but he couldn't hear me. He was, 'Get Ralph on the phone! Get him on the phone!'

Cut off from Friedgen, Ross had to call the first series of plays. Tech punted. A phone repairman came up to the Tech coaches' booth and tried to fix Friedgen's phone. It worked — for awhile. When the phones went dead again, Friedgen went wild.

Ralph Friedgen is a big, balding guy with bad teeth and as good an offensive mind as you'll find in college football. His voice booms, and his temperament is fiery enough that if his last name were Kramden instead of Friedgen, he would do Jackie Gleason proud. When the phones kept malfunctioning, Friedgen kept voicing his displeasure — first at the Tech graduate assistant coaches seated in the rear of the coaches' booth, then unwittingly at the Virginia crowd below him. When Friedgen suspected a GA had moved and disconnected him yet again, he went ballistic in a tirade as loud as it was profane. This greatly amused the media in the press box. The coaches' booth, adjacent to the press box, is encircled by clear plastic. But there's no roof. So Friedgen's fuming spilled out into the air, into the press box as well as down into the big-money, dignified old Virginia alums just a few feet below him. The UVa fans swiveled in their seats to see where this stuff was coming from; the press, knowing the source, roared. And Friedgen kept it coming.

"It was like that AT&T commercial, 'Hello, Rangoon,'" Friedgen said later. At the time, though, it seemed like "Goodbye Tech." But with phone service restored and Georgia Tech driving at last, Friedgen called a pass play on third down. He anticipated Virginia in man-to-man coverage and anticipated tailback Jeff Wright would be wide open coming out of the backfield. Wright was held up, though, and when Shawn Jones looked for him, Wright couldn't be found.

"Here's where Shawn's intelligence comes in," said Friedgen. "He knows it's man coverage. He knows Jeff's gonna be wide open. He looks for Jeff and he's not there. But he also knows with man coverage, there's nobody is on Shawn. So when Jeff's not there, he goes POOF! right up the middle and breaks for a touchdown.

Shawn Jones runs for his life, and touchdown, against Virginia.

"Same thing happened in the Citrus Bowl. First long run, he came out and the guy had his foot, and he saw they had man coverage and they had four guys to one side of the field. He knew right now he could run the football because everybody had run off with somebody else. When you've got five receivers and five guys covering them, nobody on the quarterback, he's gonna have a big play. So, it makes it not only a great athletic play, it makes it a sharp play. Shawn's sharp and gets us back in the game."

Virginia, though, responded with — what else? — another big play, this time a 44-yard Moore-to-Moore connection that set up Shawn Moore's second 1-yard TD. When they reconnected on a two-point conversion, it was 21–7. And back on the Tech sideline, the Jackets' defense was, in Ken Swilling's words, "Very bewildered. But we never lost confidence in ourselves. We talked about just holding on and making something happen. That's something that carried us through the season: no matter what happened, we never lost our poise."

Again, Shawn Jones responded. This time, he threw a 43-yard scoring pass to Jerry Gilchrist. For the Tech track sprinter-turned-flanker, it was his first career TD in just his second season of collegiate football. With Shawn Moore throwing and tailback Terry Kirby rushing, though, Virginia moved 62 yards and scored again, this time on a 6-yard keeper by Moore just 36 seconds before halftime to make it 28–14. Virginia had scored on all five of its possessions.

For Georgia Tech, halftime was a dizzying array of doubt, adjustments and hope. Joe Siffri was anything but optimistic. Early on, he hadn't felt overly emotional, "'Cause I knew we were gonna lose the way we were playing." At halftime, his hopes were, unlike Herman Moore, guarded.

"I don't wanna be embarrassed," Siffri told himself. "9–1–1 is not that bad. I don't want a runaway and mess up everything we'd worked for."

Others didn't share his pessimism. O'Leary stressed to his defense that Virginia's big plays must be stopped. Ross was

JACK WILKINSON

growing confident in the offense, but told the Jackets they weren't playing as hard as they were capable of doing. "We gotta play harder," he stressed. "We're gonna move the ball."

Friedgen told his offense that he'd overestimated Virginia's secondary, that the Jackets could throw on UVA, especially the way Jones was playing. Now, if only the Tech defense could force a turnover on the first series of the second half, then the offense must capitalize.

"Little did I know it would be the first play," said Friedgen. "And here's where the divine guidance comes in. The guy who knocks the ball out of Moore's hand is his offensive tackle."

Indeed, on the first play from scrimmage of the second half, Shawn Moore kept on an option to the right side. As he turned upfield, tackle Paul Collins—forced into the backfield by Coleman Rudolph's charge—inadvertently kicked the football from Moore's grasp. Linebacker Calvin Tiggle, who was magnificent all day with 18 tackles, recovered at the Virginia 28.

"For two years, that stuff happened against us," said Mike Mooney. "The other team got that break. This year, it happened for us."

In the huddle, Mooney recalled, the Tech offense collectively yelled, "This is it!"

And it was—just the beginning. After Tech picked up a first down, Gilchrist scored again, this time on a 12-yard, flanker-reverse-right on which he was so open, he could have walked in and seemed to be seeking defenders to juke. Just for appearances' sake. But not before a rare phone exchange between Friedgen and Ross.

When Friedgen suggested the reverse, Ross demurred. "Oh, Ralph," Ross said, "I don't know. Is it there?" Friedgen summoned up some bluster.

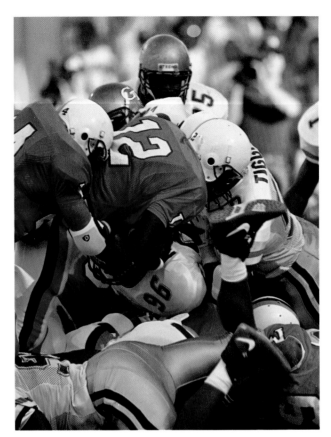

Calvin Tiggle stops Virginia—again.

"And confidently I say, 'Coach, if it wasn't there, I wouldn't call it,'" Friedgen said, laughing. "I don't know if it was there. It felt right at the time."

It felt indescribably delicious when Gilchrist scored. It was now 28–21, and now, once again, it was Calvin Tiggle time.

The wonderful thing about Tiggle is Tiggle's a wonderful big-play guy in big games. This time, a Shawn Moore pass ricocheted off Nikkie Fisher's helmet and into the grateful arms of Tiggle at the 10. He returned it 38 yards up the right sideline, in front of a roaring Tech bench, until Moore knocked him out of bounds at the Tech 48.

But there, Tech sputtered. On third and 2, the largest crowd in Scott Stadium history—all 49,700 of them—roared so

Shawn Jones came of age against Virginia.

loudly that Jones couldn't call signals. He raised up from behind the center and appealed to the officials, but they merely penalized Tech for delay of game. The Jackets' were forced to punt, but that didn't fluster Jones. He was still calm and confident.

"You have to be," Jones said. "I'm not one of those who jump up and down. That's me. You always have to direct, think ahead, show some poise."

By this time, Jones, in his words, was having "a lot of fun." Life got giddier for him after a Virginia punt. This time, Jones took Tech to the tying touchdown. It came on a 26-yard post pattern to Emmett Merchant, who made a gorgeous catch, tumbling back into the end zone after the ball bounced off his facemask. It was a play especially designed for Virginia.

"Every time we dragged the tight end [across the middle], their free safety jumped him," said Friedgen. That would isolate the speedy Merchant one-on-one with the left corner. Tech had run the play unsuccessfully earlier in the game, when Jones was pressured. This time, the protection, pattern and pass were all perfect.

At 28–28, Shawn Jones stepped out of character. He jogged to the sideline, then headed for the Tech defense and beseeched it to stop Virginia, just stop the Cavs, and he would lead Tech to another score. "Y'all just keep playing ball; we're gonna win," McClary recalls Jones saying. That startled the defenders and got their attention. Fast. Jones seldom talks like that during games and rarely to the defense. "So," said McClary, "we had to win."

It's even rarer when Jones blames or criticizes a teammate. He'll always accept the blame, though, even when the responsibility isn't his.

"That's something you have to do," Jones said. "It's his fault but I'm gonna take the blame and make him feel better. A lot of times, a person makes a mistake, you jump a guy, he's like, 'Hey, I didn't mean to do it.' I remember in high school, our coach would jump a guy and he'd go downhill."

But Jones, he elevates and inspires. "As much as he's a great athlete, the thing that makes Shawn Jones unbelievable is, he's a winner," said Mike Mooney. "He's got great physical skills. But he's not the greatest thrower and he's not the greatest runner. But at certain times, he always does something that he's never done before and at a time in a game that was so important. When we went into the Virginia game, people were talking about Shawn Moore for Heisman. I thought, 'Why not Shawn Jones?' His stats may be a little less but we hadn't lost yet.

"Shawn's the heart and soul of our team. Look, we're running an option passing attack, which is unheard of. Colorado tries to do it; they try to throw, but not like Shawn. We can go with a 10-step drop or we can run the option. There's no other quarterbacks who can do that. Maybe, Shawn Moore. But going into that game, I'd want Shawn Jones as my quarterback. I couldn't believe all the Heisman hype Shawn Moore was getting and Shawn Jones was, like, 'He's just starting to get his feet wet.' It's ridiculous. He was unbelievable that game. He went from a good quarterback to a great quarterback in that game. And he was great from that point on."

Jones's budding greatness manifested itself in many ways that day. He was calm, yet in command. "He was a sophomore in the huddle with a lot of old guys, and he was in control when the game came down to it," said Mooney. "Toughness-wise, and spiritually and leadership-wise during the week, we had Darryl and Joe and Lav. But you put three minutes left on the clock, Shawn is gonna do what has to be done."

Even earlier that day, though, Jones indelibly impressed Friedgen with his poise, judgment and restraint. Tied at 28, Shawn Moore responded with yet another bomb to Herman Moore, this a 63-yard TD that gave Virginia its last lead at 35–28. Tech's defensive problems were in part due to Ken Swilling's injury.

"That was another coaching mistake," Ross said. "I shouldn't have played Ken. He wasn't at full speed and didn't get to work [practice] like you need to for a team like Virginia. He was mentally ready to play and really wanted to, but he just wasn't physically ready. But I was looking for a spark, something that could lift us. To his credit, there are very few guys who would have come back and played in that game. It was on turf, harder on your joints, tougher on your ankles."

"A lot of people said, 'Why did you play in that game? You were hurt and you were going against Herman Moore and he was 100 percent and you were nowhere near 100 percent," said Swilling, who'd practiced only twice that week. "I felt like I needed to be there. It wasn't a point of me being out there to stop Herman Moore. I felt I needed to be there for my teammates. I feel like a lot of my teammates had a lot of confidence and trust in me."

Jones promptly rallied Tech yet again, driving the Jackets 74 yards, the final eight coming on a bullish burst through the left side by William Bell. Earlier in the week, Bell, Jones and Tom Covington were watching game films of the '89 Virginia game, in which the Jackets ran that same play. That year, Covington went in motion and the tight end missed his block. Watching the film, Covington looked squarely at Bell and assured him he'd make the block in Charlottesville. The defender Covington was supposed to block would be the right corner, Tony Covington.

"He was talking trash all week," Bell said, "and Tom said he'd make the block this time. You could just look in his face and see that he was serious."

True to his word, Covington crushed Covington and Bell ran over a defender at the goal line to score and tie it.

Tech held and Jones had the Jackets moving again. On third and long, Friedgen called for a pass play. Jones threw the ball away, but Tech still had its first lead at 38–35 on Scott Sisson's 32-yard field goal midway through the fourth quarter. Jones came off the field, immediately picked up the phone and apologized to Friedgen. "Coach, I'm sorry I had to throw it away," Jones said. "There was nobody open." Friedgen beamed.

"Shawn, I've been trying to get you to do that for two years," Friedgen said. "You put us in the lead. It's 38–35. They've got to beat us now. You try to make a play there, they intercept, it's a tie game."

"That's when I saw Shawn start to grow," Friedgen recalled. "Because he knows he can take a shot like that now and still put us in position. Don't take points off the board. And, what I really liked about it was, it was in a pressure situation."

The pressure was never greater, though, than that which the Georgia Tech defense then faced. Again, Shawn Moore riddled the Jackets and directed Virginia to the Tech 1, first and goal. The subsequent six-play sequence is the stuff of legend. As the Cavaliers came to the line, Kevin Battle heard their linemen calling, "Here we come! Coming in, coming in!"

First down: Nikki Fisher stopped for no gain.

Then: Virginia penalized five yards for illegal procedure.

Second down: Shawn Moore to Herman Moore for five more yards. Third and goal at the 1.

"We knew if they scored on that one, we were pretty much out of it," said Jeremiah McClary. But the Jackets were buoyed by the memory of their goal line stand against Clemson. Said McClary, "It was like, 'We held the No. 1 rushing team in the country out, we can hold Virginia out.'"

Third down: An apparent TD pass, Moore dumping over the middle to tight end Aaron Mundy. "When they scored, they were hollering, shooting us birds and stuff like that," said Battle. "Then I looked over and saw the flag and went, 'Yeah, yeah, yeah!' I was hoping it was against them."

It was. Virginia had had just six men on the line of scrimmage. Again, illegal procedure. Again, third down, this time at the 6. And as he gathered himself one more time, Coleman Rudolph asked himself, "Is this series ever going to end?"

Not until Tiggle somehow covered Herman Moore, and covered himself with glory again. Taking a short drop, Shawn Moore fired over the middle a fastball, low and away, toward Moore. Having already caught one pass on his knees, Moore stretched out his sinewy frame and prepared to gather in the ball. But Tiggle cut him off at the almost-perfect pass, diving and reaching and somehow, at the last instant, tipping the pass away.

It was a magnificent effort, a mental snapshot for the ages. With 2:34 to place, Virginia was forced to settle for a tying field goal. And then Jones, Bell and Sisson stepped to the fore. Friedgen, too. Hello, Rangoon? Nah. Goodbye, Virginia.

"I had this play in mind that I wanted to call in the drive, but I don't know why I called it the first place," said Friedgen. "It just came out of my mouth because I was thinking of doing something else."

The play is called 7–72. It's a pass play and Jones' first option — depending on the coverage — is Bell, slipping out of the back-

In the second half, Tech finally slowed down the Cavs.

field and running a seam pattern straight up the middle. All game, Virginia's secondary had been in a three-deep coverage. Now, in an apparent two-minute drill situation, Virginia went two deep: the two safeties splitting the field in half and providing deep help for the two corners. Virginia had done a good job all day of disguising its coverages. But as Tech broke the huddle (in which the Jackets had all held hands and encouraged each other) and came to the line, Friedgen immediately saw the coverage and said aloud in the booth, "We've got a chance for a big play."

It was all dependent upon Jones's recognition. Bingo: Jones saw what Friedgen saw. Two-deep. As he dropped back, Jones looked to his right to freeze the safety deep to that side, knowing all the while he'd look back over the middle for Bell, slipping behind a linebacker. When the play was first called, Bell sensed he'd be open, reasoning, "I knew none of the linebackers would stick with me."

Bell was indeed open, but only momentarily, only until the safety, once the ball was released, converged on him. "I tried to touch the ball to William and he made a great catch," said Jones. "You throw the ball at someone's helmet, you say, 'Good pass.' But it's a tough catch."

"Shawn just laid it up perfect and I caught it," said Bell. "And I knew I had to hold onto it." Indeed, Bell had had difficulty holding onto the ball since injuring his right thumb earlier in the day. On the cover of the next week's *Sports Illustrated,* there was Bell, carrying the ball beneath the headline, "The Sting." Clearly, his injured right thumb is bent far backward.

On this play, though, Bell held onto the ball, gaining 23 yards to the Tech 47. Not so the next play, however. Friedgen called for a split-back alignment, hoping Virginia would expect another pass. Sure enough,

Virginia dropped back into pass coverage as Jones dropped back, only to hand to Bell on a draw. "Here," Friedgen said, "is where divine guidance comes in again."

Bell gained 13 yards. He also fumbled. "I really didn't get tackled," Bell said. "I kind of fell and as I was falling, the ball came out, and I did not want to keep going. So I just kind of fell awkwardly to stop myself from rolling forward. And as I fell, I rolled back trying to get the ball back and it just so happened when I rolled over to get it, the ball bounced up and I grabbed it."

Later, Bell would tell Friedgen he was scared to death when he fumbled. On the sideline, Ross never saw the ball bounce free. The Tech offensive line did, though, and several linemen covered up Bell once he'd recovered. Back in the huddle, the Jackets shouted, "No one fumble the ball — and we will score!"

During all this, the phones went pfffft again, and Friedgen had a fit again. Two plays later, on third and 5 at the Virginia 35, Jones dropped back again. Tech never lost its poise on that final drive, never even resorted to its two-minute drill. This time, Jones hit Greg Lester, who ran a gorgeous pattern. He cut inside the corner, curled back inside around the linebacker, caught the ball, then quickly accelerated upfield for another seven yards for a 15-yard gain. Ball at the UVa 20. Now Sisson was in field goal range.

Virginia tried to rattle Sisson, calling consecutive timeouts. What appeared to be a high-level strategy session was unfolding on the Tech sideline. In actuality, running back coach Danny Smith, at offensive line coach Pat Watson's urging, wondered if Ross wanted to calm down Sisson.

"Calm him down?!" Ross said. "What the hell am I gonna say to him now?"

Watson suggested a joke. Ross didn't know any. Watson did. So Ross called

Sisson over to hear Watson's joke, then walked away, laughing. "A lot of good that did," said Ross. "Scott's eyes were big as silver dollars."

But Sisson was fine. Scott Aldredge had seen to that. The punter is also Sisson's holder. When special teams coach Mark Hendrickson first approached Sisson on the sideline, Aldredge grabbed him and said, "Coach, I've got him under control, just go on."

By then, Sisson had already warmed up, kicking a few balls into the net. "Just stroke it," Aldredge advised, patting Sisson on the head.

"When I went out there, I knew we were at least tied," Sisson said. "That makes you feel a lot better, going in with a tie with the No. 1 team in the nation."

As Sisson lined up his kick, many Jackets on the sideline couldn't bring themselves to watch. A circle of offensive linemen and one

quarterback — Siffri, Jenkins, Paul Bowman, Mark Hutto — grabbed each other's hands and prayed. Vociferously. "Sounded like an old Southern Baptist church: 'Oh God, praise the Lord, Lord have mercy,'" said Siffri. "We didn't care. Whatever it took."

It took just seconds — but an eternity — for Sisson's 37-yard field goal to split the uprights. Scott Stadium was deathly silent save for the 1,000 or so Tech fans. Georgia Tech 41, Virginia 38. Just seven seconds left. For Bobby Ross, an eternity. No time to celebrate. Not yet.

"I'm thinking, 'Oh boy, here we go again,'" said Ross. His mind flashed to Tech's last visit to Charlottesville in '88, when Tech took a late lead only to surrender a long kickoff return and, ultimately, a last-minute, winning field goal in Virginia's 17–16 triumph. On the delirious Tech sideline, all the veteran players were shouting, "Do

Shawn Jones brings Tech downfield one last time.

NOT let that happen! You gotta cover the kickoff! Don't let up!" The way Herman Moore was playing, anything was possible.

But not this time. Tech kicked off, and covered. When Shawn Moore let fly one final desperate prayer, Erick Fry intercepted, clinching the greatest victory in Georgia Tech history and igniting its most memorable celebration.

"Overwhelming," Willie Clay called it. "There was so much excitement and adventure in that game that I'm playing and imagining somebody watching it, and it was like one of those games I used to watch and somebody is saying, 'I want to play in a game like that.' It's once in a lifetime. A game like Virginia happens only once, maybe twice in a lifetime."

"At the end of the game, it was like a dream come true, because I had always wanted to play in a game like that."

Dreamily, deliriously, Tech celebrated on the field, players and coaches screaming and cheering, crying and hugging each other. Fans and family, too, climbed over the wall and rushed down onto the field. Clay's mother, Marsha, and little brother, Jason, hopped over the wall and came down to embrace him.

"It was like they went through that experience with me," Clay said. "It's difficult, you know. I'm from a single-parent home, and it's difficult when I can't be home at times and my Mom misses me. And for her to be there was very special to me. She was at all the big games, including the Citrus Bowl. She experienced it with me, made the plays with me while I was out there. That's the way I always feel. I will never forget she and my brother came on the field and were hugging me. And it just felt so good."

The rest of Scott Stadium, so thunderous all day, was now deathly silent. Shocked. One Tech man looked up into a private box and wondered, "What the hell could that conversation be like?" In George Welsh's private box were his wife; Georgia athletic director Vince Dooley and his wife, Barbara, whose son Derek was a starting wideout for Virginia; and ex-Tech coach and now Kentucky coach Bill Curry and his wife, Carolyn, whose son Billy was Virginia's long snapper.

Back down on the field, amidst the pandemonium, Kevin Bryant searched madly for Bus Ross. At his Tuesday press conference, Ross had said his father, 86, planned to attend the game and that coaching in front of his dad thrilled him. "This may be the last football game he sees," Ross said, then paused. "I hope he can make it." His eyes welled up and turned red, and Bobby Ross offered an apology. As if one were needed.

On Wednesday, Jay Shoop had given Bryant a post-game assignment, provided Tech won: find Bobby Ross's father and escort him to the locker room. Bryant had climbed up into the stands; when he found Alice Ross, he hugged her and asked, "Where's Bus?"

Bus Ross had already made his way down onto the field. Somehow, he made it through the madding crowd, for when Bryant finally got inside the locker room, there was Bus. There was Jay Shoop, standing near Bobby Ross and winking at Bryant. Everything would work out just fine.

For nearly an hour, players were still in their uniforms, screaming, dancing, laughing, crying and hugging each other. In lieu of champagne, Jim Lavin and others poured celebratory sodas on their teammates. Tom Covington thought of his late father, and wished he could have been there. But then, Thomas Herman Covington was, always is with his son. "This one was for you," Convington told

Scott Sisson salutes after kicking the field goal that beat Virginia.

his father as he unwrapped the tape around his wrists, the ones he always inscribes THC, his father's initials. Ironically, there were two games Covington forgot to write the initials: North Carolina and Virginia Tech.

When Bobby Ross got up to address the team — his team — Darryl Jenkins interrupted him. He explained that he and a couple of other seniors had gotten together with Jay Shoop that week, and cast an early vote on the game ball. "We decided to give it to someone very special to you," Jenkins said.

Then Jerimiah McClary introduced the recipient. With that, with Jay Shoop escorting him, players parted and a frail old man passed through them and joined his son,

At half time, Ross is concerned . . .

. . . at game's end, exultant.

JACK WILKINSON

who was already weeping. Bus Ross was helped up onto a chair. He, too, was crying, overcome with emotion. His son warmly advised, "Now just thank 'em. Don't get into a long talk. They wanna get outta here." But moved by the moment, Bus Ross talked, and talked some more. He finally stepped down, but not before saying, "You have made a very old man very happy."

And this: "From the bottom of my heart, this is one of the greatest things to happen to me."

The game ball, his trophy, now sits proudly on Bus Ross' dining room table, with a ribbon tied around it and bearing the final score and the inscription, "To Mr. Ross, from the Georgia Tech Football Team."

For those who were there, the memory remains, vivid and everlasting, an elderly father standing there, clutching a football, and his son beside him, weeping for joy. "It was like standing still in time," said Kevin Bryant. "Those moments are few and far between. I just stood there and said to myself, 'This is something I'll remember all my life.' "

Later that evening, Bryant, Ross and all the Jackets would savor another unforgettable experience. After the game, Ross, shouting above the raucous locker room din in a voice grown hoarse, had proclaimed, "I think we're back. I'll admit it, we're finally back. I've been reluctant to say that."

"I thought we were," Ross says now, "but I said it more for them because I wanted them to hear it, and believe it."

Incredibly, yet completely, Georgia Tech football was back. Waiting back in Atlanta, though, was an experience as memorable and meaningful as the Virginia game itself.

The flight home rivaled the Maryland flight. Some Jackets missed out, though; some 15–20 players who didn't make the traveling squad drove to Charlottesville, some to dress out, others in sweats, even though they wouldn't be playing. "That's how close that team was," said Mooney, "how focused we were in practice for that game. While they were driving back to Atlanta that night, their teammates savored something special in the air.

This was truly the flight of the phoenix, a once-proud program that had completely risen from the ashes. Now the Jackets partied hearty on the plane, singing, dancing, calling each other by name to strut their stuff in the aisle, then calling upon coaches and even Homer Rice to "Come on, Homer, get up and show us your stuff!" Unfazed by dance fever, Rice declined. But the players roared, and reveled in the glow of victory.

"It was a very warm feeling," said Covington. "We have just made a nice statement to the nation, accomplished something people thought we couldn't. And there was deep satisfaction within ourselves, just a joyous feeling. You really didn't know what you wanted to do — party, hug each other. It was just euphoria, just mind-boggling: 'Wow, we did it! We're on our way! Our undefeated season is coming into focus. Our destiny.' "

When the Tech charter landed at Hartsfield, a couple of hundred fans were there to greet the Jackets. That was nice, if predictable. Upon boarding the team buses for the return to campus, a couple of players said, "Wonder if there's gonna be any students there?" A policeman on the offensive team bus tried to prepare them, telling Mooney and the others, "There's tons of people there." Not surprisingly, the Jackets were skeptical. When the bus turned onto North Avenue, though, there was a huge crowd up at The Varsity. Mooney wondered, "Why are they here? It's late."

As the buses approached campus, players noticed a roadblock at the corner of North

Avenue and Techwood Drive. When Shawn Jones saw dozens of police officers — including Atlanta police chief Eldrin Bell — "I thought there was a fight or something." And then the buses turned left onto Techwood.

And there they were. Thousands and thousands of Georgia Tech students and fans. They'd been there for hours, ever since game's end, singing and drinking and dancing in the street. Now the objects of their affection had finally arrived, and the street party erupted anew.

There were so many people, the buses couldn't budge for several minutes. To Lavin, a New Orleans native, "It reminded me of Mardi Gras and we were the parade coming down the street. You just had people 15 and 20 deep, people standing on the ledges in front of the dorms. Just wall-to-wall people, and madness, hysteria."

To Shawn Jones, this sea of humanity was "like that square in China." Tienanmen Square, in Beijing. Kevin Battle immediately thought, "World War III." Jerimiah McClary estimated the crowd at 10,000.

As students continued to stream out of the dorms and join the crowd, the buses slowly, slowly made their way down Techwood Drive. Bobby Ross still remembers one guy, somehow stuck on the front of the bus, clinging to the windshield. "Like a monkey," Ross said. "I'm thinking, 'How in the hell is he holding on?'"

Ross also was thinking this: "It amazed me. I never thought that would happen at Georgia Tech. I'd seen it happen at Maryland, when we beat North Carolina when they were No. 2. But I'd never seen that here."

This was New Year's Eve in Times Square times 10. In their joyous zeal, the crowd accidentally cracked some windows on the buses. When the buses finally made their way down the street near the players' entrance in Grant Field, the crowd was so frenzied and squished up against the buses, it took three minutes before the doors could even be opened. Champagne came spraying through open windows. When the door to the defensive bus could finally open, McClary was the defensive guinea pig. The first one off the defense bus.

Wisely, he gathered himself and dove into the crowd, all 279 pounds of him. "I didn't touch the ground for three minutes," McClary said. The crowd just passed him around, a life-size, living, breathing, laughing, 279-pound beach ball. As other players exited, they, too, were engulfed by the fans. "As soon as you got off the bus, you got mugged," said Jones. "It was a given. It was great."

Fans cheered players, hugged them, slapped their backs, shook their hands, kissed them, got their autographs. And sprayed them with various fluids of undetermined origin. "I think I got splashed with all kinds of liquids," said Lavin. "It was great. I messed up my suit and everything."

Bobby Ross had been the first one off the first bus. He, too, had a major concern: His luggage. "Daddy! Daddy!" Ross heard when he stepped off the bus. It was his youngest child, Robbie, a student at Marist High School and now part of the crowd. Ross kept fretting over his luggage, and his wife. Kevin Bryant rushed up to Ross and yelled, "Forget your luggage! Just get on out!"

And to himself, Bryant said this after watching Ross leave the bus and the crowd let leave of its senses and go ballistically bananas: "This is it. He sees, he really sees. They really care! This is like something out of a World Series."

The Jackets had already heard the music, seen the fire and smelled the smoke. Once

JACK WILKINSON

out of the bus and into the street, they had an up-close view of the bonfire of the insanities. Immediately after the game ended, hundreds of Tech students had flicked off their TVs and rushed outside and into Grant Field. There, they tore down both goal posts and paraded their trophies in the streets. Then one goal post was fed to a victory pyre at the intersection of Bobby Dodd Way and Techwood Drive. The fiery pyre was fueled by old couches and chairs and bed frames from dormitories; it had grown so intense, so high, the traffic lights hanging above started to melt. "Maybe someone learned something about thermodynamics," Georgia Tech president Dr. John Patrick Crecine said two days later. "Heat rises."

But the strangest sight was perched on the concourse in front of the main entrance to the Edge Athletic Center. There stood the lone stranger, shirtless, with long, stringy black hair and an enormous amplifier, strumming a guitar and singing a solo version of Deep Purple's "Smoke on the Water." Indeed, there was smoke on the corner, and fire in the sky. And inside every Tech player and coach lay an even warmer glow.

"That was when I knew the whole campus was with us," said Mike Mooney. "Everybody wanted us to win then, everybody was watching us. That's when I knew everybody knew we were gonna do something big.

"Getting off that bus, it wasn't just young little kids. It was older men and women, people 50 years old. I've never been part of the Tech tradition back in the early 50s. I've met a lot of those guys. I could tell

Ross greeted by welcoming committee on return to Tech campus.

"Bonfire of the Insanities" in celebration of huge win over Virginia.

they were tough men. Coach Ross brings some of them from the 1952 national championship team to talk to us, like George Morris, and they had an aura about them. You knew, 'He must have been a great player.' You could tell that he was tough. Then you see all those people out there, there were some of those guys there. There were people from everywhere. It's a feeling I'll probably never have again, but I'll never forget it, either. If I had to play a last college football game, if I ever had to choose one, that would be it."

"It was the best thing that could have happened to this school," said Willie Clay. "The best."

"It's one of those things you can only feel from sports," said Shawn Jones.

"It was a total shock," said Tom Covington. "To see so many people so into the game, and everybody eventually come out. And they'd been out there hours . . ."

"Even the studying type," said Kevin Battle.

". . . All helping you celebrate in our victory," continued Covington. "And it was our victory—theirs, ours, Tech's victory. We couldn't believe it, just sat with our mouths open. We were very geeked—so excited, elated, very hoarse. We just wanted to break out the champagne, like a celebration at the World Series or Super Bowl."

And how had all this made Jerimiah McClary feel? "Wanted," he said, laughing. His eight siblings and their children had all come down to Tech to share in his joy. "For all these years, we'd just been Georgia Tech football. Now we were getting respect, and we deserved it. Just people acknowledging us as more than athletes. We were part of Georgia Tech now. That was a great feeling."

chapter

With the victory over Virginia, Georgia Tech rose to No. 7 in the polls, its highest national ranking since 1966. The following week, all around the Edge Athletic Center, the buzz was about polls and bowls and national championship showdowns.

Now the Jackets seemed certain to win the ACC and represent the conference in the Citrus Bowl. But the ACC's agreement with the Citrus had an escape clause: if the ACC leader was ranked No. 2, 3 or 4 in the Nov. 13 UPI poll, it had the option of playing in the Orange, Sugar or Cotton bowls. In other words, Tech might well get the chance to play top-ranked Colorado for the national championship in the Orange Bowl.

Naturally, such speculation and an inevitable letdown did not bode well for Tech. Nor did its next opponent: Virginia Tech, a deceptively capable team coached by Frank Beamer, one of Bobby Ross's closest friends, a former assistant to Ross at The

Citadel and an outstanding coach himself.

"Now you're going to play a good friend of yours," said Friedgen, who was also an assistant with Beamer, "and you know he's a good football coach and it's going to be a hard game. But our kids were on cloud nine."

And on Saturday, they were wide tackle-sixed. Virginia Tech is one of the last hold-outs, Beamer one of the last coaches to employ the old wide tackle six defense. With its six-man front, so rare in contemporary football, Virginia Tech invariably presents defensive problems to most opponents — particularly those unfamiliar with the scheme and still gloating over the previous victory.

Bobby Ross's fears were well-founded. As Georgia Tech prepared to take the field at Bobby Dodd Stadium, Ross stood among his players and heard the crowd. Many were still congratulating the Jackets for their tri-

Jerrelle Williams juggles but hangs on to the interception.

umph in Virginia. That worried Ross deeply. Smart man, Bobby Ross.

And then there was the wind. It had rained Friday and with Saturday came a strong, gusting wind, and it would make life miserable for Tech. "That was a cold game," William Bell remembered. "It was very cold that day, but still the sun was out, which made you sweat. But the breeze made you cold, too."

And the combination of the sun, the wind and Virginia Tech made Georgia Tech break out in a cold sweat, literally and figuratively.

"I hate the wind," said Bobby Ross. "I'll take pouring-down rain, but I hate the wind. I think it's an equalizer. It really scares me. Not that they needed an equal-

izer, because they were a very good football team." As Florida State had already discovered (the Hokies took a two-touchdown lead at FSU before succumbing) and as Virginia would come to learn.

For the longest time, it seemed Georgia Tech's national championship hopes were gone with the wind that day. For three quarters, the Jackets did the Hokie-pokey. Scott Sisson missed second-quarter field goal attempts of 42 and 44 yards.

"He missed those first two and I have to say I was cussin' him," Ross said later that day. "But I got to remember he comes back."

Sisson got a third chance because his defense was as staunch as Virginia Tech's. The Hokies missed a first-quarter field goal

Scott Sisson signals his field goal against Virginia Tech is good.

attempt, then Keith Holmes blocked another one in the third. Virginia Tech finally took a 3–0 lead midway through the fourth quarter.

"We're in a fight for our lives," said Friedgen. "But to the kids' credit, at the end of the game, against the wind when they had to have it, they made two drives."

The first drive was an immediate response to the VPI field goal, Jones taking the Jackets 55 yards before Sisson tied the game at 3-all with a 33-yard field goal with 5:09 to play. "It was tough passing," Jones said. "The wind made the ball go down and up all day."

And Jones made the Jackets go when it counted. Chris Simmons recovered a fumble, then the teams exchanged punts before Georgia Tech took over at its 16 with but 1:10 left. Time for an abbreviated version of the two-minute drill.

"That was something we were real good on," Jones said. "We practice that. You gotta have it. On the last drive, it seemed like everybody was, 'OK, it's two minutes. It's time to get to work.' "

"I thought that was the most amazing drive we had all year long," said Bobby Ross. "That was The Drive as far as I'm concerned."

Georgia Tech had struggled all day, committing five turnovers and a season-high 44 yards in penalties. Now, though, Jones was on target. He completed four passes in the drive, first a 17-yarder to Emmett Merchant, then a 7-yard, third-and-4 to Merchant. Then came the decisive moment. Jones dropped back, slipped outside the Hokies' containment and lofted the ball to Bell. Earlier in the game, Bell had lost a contact lens. Now, with the ball hanging in the air and the game — and season — hanging in the balance, Bell leaped for the ball. Too soon.

"He misjudged his jump but just hung there, like Michael Jordan," said Friedgen. "And he caught the ball for a first down and got out of bounds."

On the next play, Jones rifled an 18-yard completion to Merchant at the VPI 23. Two plays later, Ross called on Sisson.

Said Ross, "I told him, 'Don't worry about the wind, just kick it. Don't try to guide it. Just drive it and let's see what happens.' "

Virginia Tech called two timeouts, hoping to rattle Sisson. Wrong: His 38-yarder with eight seconds left beat Virginia Tech 6–3, extended Georgia Tech's unbeaten streak to 13 games and preserved the Jackets' title hopes. After Sisson had beaten Virginia, balloons and bouquets had been sent to his parents' home in Marietta. A letter arrived from the mayor of Marietta. Now Sisson had done it again.

"That thing took off," said Ross. "He hit the hell out of the ball. That was a great kick. I don't know if I've ever seen a kick like that, as significant and difficult and under as much pressure. That was not a wind to play with. Some people say it died down when he kicked it. It did not die down. It died down when Virginia Tech called timeout. But when he kicked it, there was a gust. But when he kicked it, I said, 'My God, it's gonna be good!' 'Cause I really didn't think it was gonna make it; I really didn't."

It did. It made Tech 8–0–1 and it enabled the Jackets to jump from seventh to fourth in the AP poll. No. 2 Washington, No. 3 Houston and No. 6 Iowa all lost that day. But in the UPI poll, Georgia Tech moved up from No. 7 to 5 — one spot shy of opting for the Orange over the Citrus. Still, the Jackets had their highest ranking since 1961 as well as the nation's longest unbeaten streak. They were now 15–1–1 in their last 17 games. And they were now a victory away from winning their first ACC championship.

chapter 10

In 1986, Georgia Tech had come to Winston-Salem, N.C., in search of a seemingly certain victory and a resultant bowl bid. But when the Jackets were upset 24–21 by Wake Forest, they lost not just a football game but a bid to the Bluebonnet Bowl as well. And thus began their 16-game ACC losing streak.

This time, the Jackets assured, would be different. This time would be, in the words of Thomas "World T." Balkcom, "From worst to first." This time, Tech would transform Groves Stadium into Citrus Groves.

"A complete, fun game," Ross said, reflecting on Wake Forest. "That and the Nebraska games were the fun games."

But even in a fun game, against an opponent that was badly outmanned, Bobby Ross found something to fret about. When the Jackets checked into their hotel on Friday, they discovered, to their delight and Ross's chagrin, that a sorority was holding

its annual convention there. Ross immediately had visions of the hotel becoming the Delta house.

"Coach Ross walked in and he was, like, 'Oh, no!,'" said McClary, grimacing to mimic Ross. "All the guys were pretty vocal when we walked in and saw them. Like, 'Whew!' Coach Ross kept patrolling the lobby. In meetings, he stressed that curfew was 11 p.m. sharp.

"All the guys were enjoying the scenery, of course. But by this time, we were on a mission."

By this time, the Jackets were clearly focused on the top, determined to beat Wake Forest and win the ACC. "So we weren't about to jeopardize anything by doing something foolish like sneaking out," McClary said. "So we conversed up until it was time to go to bed and then said, 'We gotta go do something in the morning.'"

Their Wake-up call came promptly and

Bobby Rodriguez's TD catch . . .

JACK WILKINSON

. . . and TD reverse against Wake Forest.

the Jackets responded. Never mind that just 13,493 fans bothered to come out to Groves on a windy, sun-lit day. Never mind that Tech had lost three straight to Wake before prevailing in '89. Never did Tech look complacent or overconfident, at least not until it no longer mattered.

Or as Ralph Friedgen put it, "The attitude of the kids was, 'Let's not screw around, let's put these guys out early.' "

Even Mike Tyson, once a notorious early finisher, would have been impressed with Tech's voracity, and efficiency, from the outset. Once Wake won the coin toss, deferred and inexplicably went against the wind, Tech went wild. The Jackets scored twice in the first quarter, twice more in the second and took a commanding 28–0 halftime lead. In the third quarter, Ross was already emptying his bench.

"It seemed kind of boring," said Shawn Jones. "There was hardly anybody there. But you got a chance to see all your friends play.

"I sensed the coaching staff really wanted us to concentrate and not let this opportunity slip by. But I thought the players were relaxed yet confident. Then you're at your best."

After guiding the Jackets 86 yards on the first possession (culminated by William Bell's 1-yard scoring run), Jones found Bobby Rodriguez on a slant-post pattern for a 54-yard TD and 14–0 lead. After fullback Carl Lawson scored just 30 seconds into the second quarter, Rodriguez scored again, this time on a 22-yard flanker reverse. It was 28–0. And it was over.

When the captains came out before the second half began, Wake quarterback Phillip Barnhill had clearly had enough. Turning to Tech's Calvin Tiggle, Barnhill asked, "Hey, get 'em to lay off me a little bit."

Tech's defense had been as ferocious as the offense had been insatiable. Midway

through the third quarter, Bell was primed to score again from the 1. But this time, he fumbled into the end zone. And there was Jim Lavin.

"Two Wake Forest guys went for it and the ball squirted out from under them," said Lavin. "I saw it and I just dove on top of the ball. Next thing I know, I saw the official's hands go up. I had about 2,000 pounds of man on top of me, starting with 325 with Mike."

Mike Mooney, Lavin's best buddy, also dived for the ball. On the radio, Al Ciraldo and Kim King initially reported Mooney had recovered. "We both kinda had it, but Lav was like on it more," said Mooney. "So I let him go and I covered on top of him. People were coming in, like they do any time that ball's in the end zone. People are pounding on me and I'm, like, 'Lav, you got it, you got it?' He said, 'Yeah' and we both started laughing. I'm in there, I'm getting crushed, guys are sticking their helmets in my back, I'm, like, 'Jimmy, Jimmy, I'm getting killed up here.' "

"Just hold on," Lavin said.

As they finally arose, Mooney said, "Jimmy, I took all the abuse for this. There's no reason I shouldn't get some of it."

Uh-uh. Not after scoring. Not after the first, and in all likelihood the last, touchdown of Lavin's football career. "I'd never really even touched the ball," he said. "This was like the icing on the cake. So I made sure I kept the ball. I wasn't gonna give that one back, wasn't gonna let go of that ball unless I was legally forced to."

Jim Lavin kept his football. And up in the stands at Groves Stadium sat his parents, thrilled and thankful they'd been able to see their son's moment of triumph. Jim and Juanita Lavin still live in River Ridge, La., outside New Orleans and didn't get to see their son play very often. Not that they

"Mr. TD," Jim Lavin.

didn't want to: Jim Lavin played at LSU, his final season coming in 1957 — a year before LSU won the national championship. When Tech stunned Virginia, the Lavins couldn't make the trip to Charlottesville, watching instead on TV. For Wake Forest, though, they'd driven 12 hours. And now they were rewarded. Their son, too.

"If there's anyone on the team that didn't get enough credit this year, it's Lav," said Mooney. "I got noticed 'cause I was the only junior [on the offensive line]. Joe got it because he's so durable, Darryl because he's just a great football player. Our centers didn't get a lot because they were alternating. But I don't think Lav ever got the notoriety he deserved, because he did so much.

"He played everywhere, any position. You don't have guys doing that any more — playing the left side, right side, knowing every assignment any of us have to do and telling us. Sometimes in the huddle, we'll have special schemes for certain teams, change things around a little. They'll call the play and Jimmy'll tell me and Joe, 'Remember, if they're in this on that side, you gotta do this.' Sometimes we laugh at him: 'Appreciate it, Jim. We aren't good.' But he's always out there, constantly thinking. We couldn't afford to lose any of our offensive linemen, but if we lose him we're in tough shape."

In nearly as tough shape as Jim Lavin once was when he came to Georgia Tech. At Tech's football banquet in 1990, Lavin spoke of his metamorphosis on The Flats. Of how he'd once cried himself to sleep in the dorms, so miserable and misplaced was he. And now how he'd cry at the knowledge that he'd no longer play any football at this place he'd grown to love. In a way, Jim Lavin became a before-and-after poster boy for Georgia Tech football.

"I just couldn't figure out what I was doing here at Georgia Tech," said Lavin, who'd transferred after a year at Army and followed assistant coach Brian Baker to Tech. "I was away from home. For the second time, I'd chosen to go to school away from home. I missed home so bad."

Lavin was terribly homesick. He was also terribly out of place at Georgia Tech as a redshirt. Later came the infamous pizza brawl. "I didn't know why I was messing up," he said. He was cutting classes and not studying. He was late to meetings and practices, would violate team rules and break curfew.

"There was really no aspect of my life that was going forward," Lavin said. "I was just bucking the system, wasn't conforming. There were times I'd sit around and be so upset and so distraught, I'd just cry and think, 'What the heck am I doing here? What am I doing with myself?' "

Eventually, Lavin found himself, and his sense of purpose. As well as a sense of fulfillment. "Now, I look back and I'm glad I stayed," he said. "I just wish I had another year of football so bad."

No year could compare with this one, however. In the fourth quarter, Lavin and Mooney reveled with the other starters and cheered their understudies. With fully 12 minutes to play, Marco Coleman and Calvin Tiggle had already taken off their shoulder pads and were posing for photos on the Tech sideline. Pat Crecine came down to the sideline in time to see Willie Clay raise a baton and conduct the Georgia Tech pep band.

"The kids got a little rambunctious on the sideline and a couple of our coaches said something," said Ross. "I said, 'Let it go. Let 'em enjoy it. They need to enjoy it and I want 'em to. Cool it. Let 'em have their fun, as long as we're respectful to our opponents.' And we were."

"We celebrated, but we didn't want to

Tech players with ACC championship banner.

rub it in," said McClary. "Two years ago, we were like Wake Forest."

And now the Jackets were champions. Mike Williams' 83-yard interception return punctuated the 42–7 victory, giving Tech its first ACC championship and first championship of any kind in 38 years, since the 1952 SEC championship. As the clock ticked down, Thomas Balkcom suckered Ross with a congratulatory handshake, while his teammates doused their coach with a bucket of ice-cold Gatorade. Ross was carried off the field on his players' shoulders. Once inside the locker room, he congratulated his team. The Citrus Bowl extended an informal invitation. And then the young lefthander became the cigar man: Kim King distributed victory cigars. Jerimiah McClary took a few puffs and got nauseous, but Marco Coleman and several other Jackets puffed away contentedly.

"It was a fat one," said Coleman. "And I smoked it. Definitely."

"Georgia Tech is the best-balanced football team in America," said Wake Forest coach Bill Dooley. "Offense, defense, every way."

Bobby Ross enjoyed it all. Definitely. After three ACC titles at Maryland, Bobby Ross had finally won one at Georgia Tech. How did they compare?

"Complementary," Ross said. "A title is a title. Our kids at Maryland had been through some things, too. But I was very happy for our seniors, the Darryl Jenkinses and Siffris and Jerimiah McClarys and Thomas Balkcoms. There's a story behind each of those kids. Each one has been through so much. Even an Angelo Rush, who doesn't play much and who watched his brother drown while swimming. To have a family tragedy like that, and he still came through and stayed with the program and he graduated.

"That's what was so satisfying to me. I'm not trying to sound idealistic, but that's

Ross carried from field after clinching Tech's first ACC championship.

even more satisfying to me than even being named No. 1. To be able to see those kids so satisfied. To see those kids develop confidence-wise as people. It's helped 'em. And to see those kids stick with it, to understand about perseverance, to understand that if you really stick to something and work at it, and see the reward, it's got to help them immensely as people.

"Here's a group of seniors that had been through more than any group of players I've ever been around. You look at what

they've been through: Riccardo Ingram's signing, Chris Caudle's death, Dave Pasannella's death. Losing. Each of them had something individually, along with what they experienced as a team. That's what was a really good feeling to me."

Ross was also reminiscing about teams past, former players. "Back to the Jerry Mayses and Jeff Mathises," said Ross. "And the Sean Smiths and Willie Burks and the Jessie Marions, and wishing they could be there, too. Because they contributed, too."

chapter

The Wake Forest fallout was considerable. That week, Georgia Tech jumped from fourth to third in the polls. And Bobby Ross was named the ACC Coach of the Year, the second man to win the honor at two different schools. And his star was still rising: Ross was rumored to be the choice to fill the LSU coaching vacancy. Then he was the potential prime candidate should Lou Holtz leave Notre Dame. Ross was flattered but going nowhere.

On the Saturday of Thanksgiving weekend, Tech officially received its Citrus Bowl bid. On January 1st in Orlando, the Jackets would meet Nebraska. It would be Tech's first New Year's Day bowl appearance since the 1967 Orange Bowl against Florida, Bobby Dodd's last game as head coach.

Citrus representatives flew to Atlanta, along with two costumed rodents whose ears were nearly as enormous as their celebrity: Mickey and Minnie Mouse,

straight from Disney World. They posed for a photograph with Ross, whose own ears are not exactly microscopic.

"My ears are my ears and they're big enough," he said then, laughing. "This is a special night for our program. It's a special bowl, a New Year's Day bowl, a nationally-televised bowl, and we're in the entertainment capital of the world."

That same day, Miami defeated Syracuse 33–7. Yet when the next poll was announced, the Hurricanes had slipped to No. 3, supplanted by Georgia Tech, at 9–0–1 the nation's only undefeated team. Still, Ross wouldn't lobby for No. 1. He knew what lay ahead: Georgia. In Athens.

Yes, the Dogs were a struggling 4–6, young and inexperienced offensively and depleted on the defensive line by injury, arrest and academic attrition. Still, this was Georgia. This was Georgia-Georgia Tech, a fierce rivalry and even more ferocious

Mickey and Minnie come to Atlanta to invite Ross and Tech to the Citrus Bowl.

JACK WILKINSON

between the hedges in Athens. If Tech lost, the barking would be sonic, and endless. To wit: the worst Georgia team since 1962, or B.V.D. (Before Vince Dooley), was still good enough to beat Tech's best in a quarter-century.

As always, there was two weeks' worth of pre-game banter between the teams, schools and, most vociferously, fans. There were already unflattering comparisons between this Tech team and Georgia's 1980 national champions that grated on the Jackets. But this time, the pre-game hype was more uncharacteristically one-sided. Indeed, the buzz off North Avenue drowned out the barking from Athens. In years past, Jerimiah McClary recalled, Georgia fans — confident of victory — would call information, get dorm phone numbers for Tech players, and call. And call. And call.

"They'd harass us," McClary said. "That never came this year, so we're thinking, 'They must be afraid or something.' "

No packages came in the mail this time, either. Before the '89 Georgia game, a package arrived at Tech, addressed to the offensive line. The postmark: Athens. The contents: 10 pairs of oversized pink panties. There was no return address, but the Jackets were led to believe it had been sent by one of two Georgia defenders, Bill Goldberg or Hiawatha Berry.

Surely, this was just some Tekkie hoping to infuriate and motivate the Jackets. Surely, no one from Georgia would do such a thing — and certainly not a player. Why, you'd have to be incredibly dumb or arrogantly overconfident to do such a thing.

Many of the Jackets were determined to beat Georgia to muzzle the Dawgma they'd heard for so long, in so many places. Kevin Battle spoke for many:

"When they heard I was going to Tech over Miami and Georgia and all those schools, a lot of kids from my high school [M.D. Collins High] said, 'Why are you doing that? You'll never be on TV, you'll never do this, never do that, never have a ring.' So it's sort of like to lose to Georgia would be a chance for them to say, 'I told you so,' especially since I live practically down the street from all the Georgia fans. A lot of kids who graduated a year after I did went to Georgia, some basketball players, and they live around the block and in the same vicinity as I do. And I hate to walk in the mall — Shannon Mall or Greenbriar Mall — and here they come: 'Hey, who's the championship team?' I think, 'Yeah, we'll get you guys.' Now, I can walk in the malls with my ring on and say, 'Hey, who's the championship team now? We're national champs.' "

Battle couldn't say that last December, though, and Georgia Tech couldn't say for certain what to expect in Athens. Not from the Georgia fans; from the Dogs themselves.

"We didn't know what they were gonna do," said Ralph Friedgen. "We heard they were going to put Dupree [freshman Joe Dupree] at quarterback. We heard they were going to go to the wishbone. We knew they were going to blitz us on defense. We had to be ready to play and we had to stay with our game plan."

That was not easy. Not after Georgia coach Ray Goff called upon a celebrity troika for pre-game inspiration: heavyweight champion Evander Holyfield, NFL all-time rushing leader Walter Payton and the big Dawg himself, *Atlanta Journal-Constitution* columnist Lewis Grizzard all addressed the Dogs in their locker room. Some, apparently, were listening.

These 13-point under-Dogs came out in an emotional frenzy. Garrison Hearst scored on Georgia's second possession. The Dogs then capitalized on a Tech fumble for

Tech fans at the Georgia game in Athens.

JACK WILKINSON

a John Kasay field goal and a 9–0 first-quarter lead. All season long, Georgia Tech had played with its head, not over it. But now, amidst 82,122 barking and baying crazies, all fueling the suddenly tenacious and taunting Dogs, Tech lost its composure.

The Jackets taunted back. They lost control. Jim Lavin was assessed an unnecessary roughness penalty after pulling a late-arrival, piling-on Bulldog off a pileup.

"I've never seen a team so high as Georgia," said Bobby Ross.

"They probably could have run a car off the emotion they were playing with," said Lavin.

Ralph Friedgen saw the makings of Armageddon. Tech had sputtered offensively. Shawn Jones, taking too shallow a drop-back in the face of the Georgia blitz and throwing the ball too low, had three of his first five passes knocked down at the line of scrimmage and a fourth batted away by Georgia safety Mike Jones, his brother. After Tech's second possession, Friedgen reached Jones on the sideline phone and told him, "We can't panic in this situation. We've got 'em riled up. They're going nuts. We lose our poise right now, we're going to lose this football game. Shawn, I want you to go over to the bench, tell the guys to keep their poise and let's get this next one in. No screwing around."

Darryl Jenkins and Joe Siffri had already spoken to their fellow offensive linemen. Their words were heeded. "They don't just talk to talk," said Mike Mooney. "That's why people listen to them. Joe is not a man of a lot of words, anyway. Darryl doesn't talk a bunch. But when they said something, everybody listened. That's what made them such great leaders."

Bobby Ross sought to calm his players, too. "Look, you're playing their game, you're doing what they want you to do," he

Coleman Rudolph sacks Bulldog Joe Dupree.

JACK WILKINSON

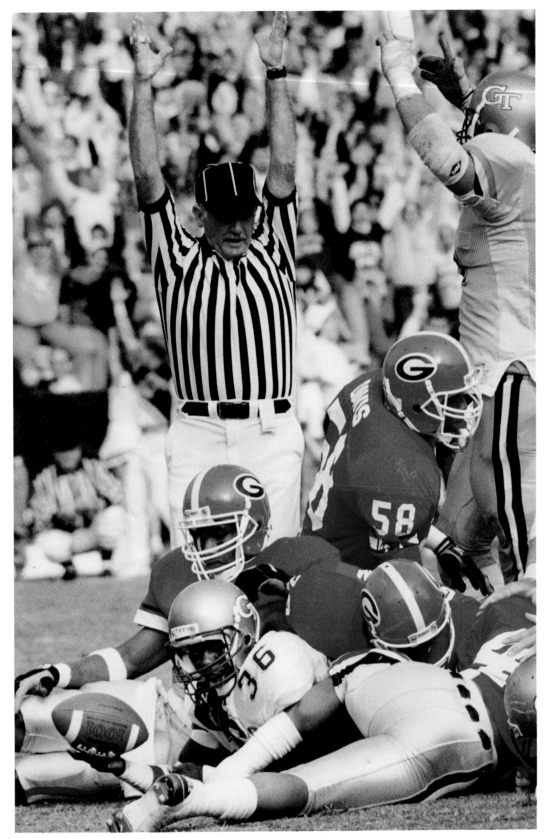

William Bell sneaks across for the score.

Bobby Rodriguez's catch put Tech ahead for good . . .

JACK WILKINSON

told the Jackets. "You've gotta get back to doing things you're supposed to do and focus on the things you're supposed to do."

And just like that, everything started coming into focus.

First Jones guided Tech 49 yards to score, the final yard coming care of William Bell. The drive was set up when a Scott Aldredge punt was downed at the 1. Initially, Bobby Ross considered going for it on fourth down when Ralph Friedgen told Ross it was fourth and one. Ross noticed the scoreboard read fourth and four, double-checked with Friedgen and, as the first quarter expired, Ross opted to punt. Presto. "It was so ironic," Ross said. "The last time we played over there, our kicking game stunk."

Bell soon scored. He would gain 128 yards for the day, thanks in part to the offensive line, Jones' effective passing and also the blocking of Captain Book Bag. That's Tech's nickname for fullback Stefen Scotton, who blocks nearly as well as he studies. Early on on The Flats, Scotton was always seen on campus carrying his textbooks in his book bag. Hence, the nickname. Hence, his 3.4 GPA in electrical engineering and his status as a two-time academic All-America.

Shawn Jones has a nickname, too: Big Toe. His size 14 shoes often caused Jones to stump his toes. Tom Covington simply calls Jones "Klutzy" away from football. But on the field, Jones is pure grace, and never moreso than this day in Athens.

This time, Tech struck quickly. First Bell gained 26 yards on an option pitch to the right, or short, side. Upstairs, Friedgen noticed the Georgia free safety came up to make the tackle. This time, Friedgen called for a play-action pass. This time, Jones faked the same option look to the right, dropped and fired left and long to Bobby Rodriguez, running a post pattern. The cornerback played it well, never allowing Rodriguez inside. But Rodriguez adjusted smartly, cutting it upfield. Jones adjusted perfectly, too, laying the ball up and over the top to Rodriguez, who made a beautiful catch while falling into the end zone. Friedgen and the other offensive assistants had spent six hours devising a two-point play specifically for Georgia. When he called it, Jones came to the line, checked off and calmly hit Greg Lester to put Tech up for good 15–9.

"I felt the entire time that once we got started playing our game, we'd be all right," said Jones. But this performance wasn't just all right. It was All-American in caliber.

Jones completed a school-record 12 straight passes (15 of 20 total for 225 yards and four touchdown passes). He led Georgia Tech to touchdowns on five consecutive possessions, spanning just 18:36. When Jones hit Emmett Merchant for a 21-yard TD and then walked in himself for a two-point conversion, the Jackets had scored 23 points in just 15 plays.

As the half expired, John Kasay's second field goal trimmed it to 23–12. Jones, however, was merely warming up. After Ken Swilling stripped the ball and Jerrelle Williams recovered at the Georgia 48, Jones made backup tight end James MacKendree's lone reception of the year a memorable one: a 7-yard TD pass. Then Jones again found Rodriguez, who finished with six catches for 119 yards. This time, it was a 25-yard scoring pass that made it 37–12.

"It just felt like everything was clicking," said Jones. "I felt like I couldn't do anything wrong, but don't make a mistake. I felt like I could gamble but don't gamble too much."

On Tech's third touchdown, Jones saw the Georgia corner right on Merchant's left hip. So he nonchalantly put the ball on Merchant's right hip. Touchdown. "I felt

. . . which called for a celebration with Emmett Merchant.

JACK WILKINSON

comfortable the entire game," Jones said. "Something about playing on the road, with a big crowd booing. There's something about challenges. I love to rise to the occasion. Even when I played basketball and teams played me box-and-one, I rose to the occasion."

"Shawn's somebody on the team who, no matter who you are—coach, player or trainer—you look at him and you respect him for what he does and not what he says," said Jerimiah McClary. "I think that's his strongest point. He doesn't go out and say, 'I'm gonna do this, I'm gonna do that.' He does it. And you say, 'That's Shawn.' "

"With Shawn, I know I've got a guy who can make plays, and he's a winner," said Friedgen. "He continues to get better. He's a very coachable kid. He just seems to be at his best when you have to have him. He will make mistakes, but he has the confidence to just not let it bother him and to overcome them. In the real good players that I've been around—the Boomer Esiasons, Shawn Joneses, Kenny Andersons, Dennis Scotts—if they're not being successful it never affects the rest of their game. They're going to take that winning shot even when they are 0 for 18. Shawn's like that.

"He has more pressure with the media than he does with the defense. He doesn't like to talk to the media. He doesn't like to talk to me. He's just an introverted kid. But he's a good kid. He's just not one of these kids that likes the spotlight. He likes his privacy and to do what he likes to do. That's him; you're not going to change that.

"The other thing I think those type of players have is an ability to absorb blame when it's not even there. For a quarterback, it's really important if a player's not successful for the quarterback to say, 'Don't worry about it, it's my fault,' even though it may not be. It's a settling effect, as opposed to saying, 'Come on, you gotta get it right.'

Shawn does that, says, 'My bad.' And he does a good job of saying, 'Good blocking,' or 'Great catch.' Kids respond to that better than the other way. If he ever did face up to them, they would go, 'Whoa!' because I've never heard him say anything or jump a guy."

Of course, in Athens there was never any call for that. "When you look at the film from the Georgia game, Shawn is textbook," Friedgen said. "He's just, like, everything is on balance and he's throwing it with his hips and it's right there. His first year his problems were mechanical, and decision-making, to a point. When he really threw a ball poorly, he wouldn't set his feet. He would throw off the wrong foot. We just worked very, very hard on his mechanics, and now even when he's not perfectly right mechanically, he still throws the ball better than he did last year.

"There's not many guys that can throw it like he did in the Georgia game, or Nebraska game. Hopefully, he can continue to grow. He's a pretty good athlete and tremendous competitor. I think people are going to hit him up with the Heisman deal and I think that's another hurdle we've gotta overcome. I don't believe in promoting guys for that. Not that I don't want to see him win it, it's just I don't think we are in a situation where we're gonna build him up or create stats for him so he can win that thing. If he's lucky enough to win the Heisman, it'll be because we were successful as a team."

If Homer Rice had a Heisman vote, he might have voted for Jones last season simply off his performances against Wake Forest, Georgia and Nebraska. "My specialty was training and coaching quarterbacks," Rice said. "I saw things in that kid and said, 'My gosh, we have a super human being!' And the way things were being put together; when you have that, you have a

Shawn Jones prepares to riddle Georgia a fourth time.

chance to beat anybody. Even against Virginia Tech, Shawn got us in position to win.

"He's a Heisman candidate. He's a first-round draft pick. He has all the tools. He's a great competitor. The last three games last year, I'd say, 'Is he gonna do it again?' God, yes. I was awestruck by the way he played."

So was Georgia. When the Bulldogs narrowed it to 37–23 early in the fourth quarter, Jones coolly commanded a 15-play, 75-yard drive. It consumed 8:06 and culminated in Scott Sisson's 22-yard field goal with just 2:41 left. As the headline in the next day's *Atlanta Journal-Constitution* advised, "Bee-lieve: Tech 40–23."

With that, Georgia Tech had rung up the highest score by an opponent in Sanford Stadium since Maryland's 43–7 win in 1951 — 440 games ago. With that, the

Jackets were 10–0–1, Tech's first unbeaten regular season in 38 years, the sixth 10-win season in school history and the first since 1956. With that, Tom Stinson wrote in the *Journal-Constitution,* "Many of them paused to tug at the hedge as they filed out the northeast gate, snapping off sprigs of real evidence from a most unreal campaign."

Jerimiah McClary and Kevin Peoples waved branches of hedge to the crowd. Marco Coleman chewed on a victory sprig as he walked into the lockerroom. Darryl Jenkins appeared to be starting a hedge farm.

And Bobby Ross glowed. "People may never know all we went through," he said. "It's a helluva thing for us."

Most people didn't know all Joe Siffri went through, either. Now, they would. On

Ken Swilling knows who's Number One.

the way home from Athens, Siffri and an uncle stopped for a steak dinner. By the time Siffri returned to his parents' house in Doraville, it was too late. His father, Charles, had finally died in his home at 7:30 that evening.

Charles Siffri was a Tech grad, in civil engineering. The last time he had seen his son play in person was 1988. In August of '89, suffering from cancer of the spine, Siffri was left partially paralyzed from surgery and chemotherapy. He was still able to see his son play football on TV, though. And more important, he was still able to see his son in person. Often.

By the start of the 1990 season, Joe Siffri was coping well with his father's illness. During the two-a-days of fall camp, when summer school was still in session, practices were held at 6 a.m. and 6 p.m. Each morning, Joe Siffri arose at 4:45. Twice weekly, he'd drive to Doraville after lunch to see his father, then nap before returning for a 3:30 team meeting, a 4:30 class and practice. Bed check at 11, start all over again six hours later.

Once the season began, Siffri went home two or three times weekly, and always on Sunday mornings, to see his dad. "He was really excited," Siffri said. "It helped him out, too. Thank God this season we were on TV a lot. He got to see most of the games on TV. He was actually sharing it with me and it brought him some joy."

Once Charles Siffri was bedridden, his wife Sheila got a lift to help get him out of bed. Then she'd put her husband in the living room to watch their son on TV. And he would glow with paternal pride.

The day before the Georgia game, Joe Siffri called home. "Come home right after the game," his mother told him. Charles Siffri was terminally ill. Doctors had told the family he might live until March of '91. "But my mom knew," said Joe Siffri. "Still,

it shocked me when I got home."

Charles Siffri had had a bad day, the last one he'd endure. The end started right around game time. By halftime, Sheila had to turn the TV off. By 7:30, he was gone.

"What Joe went through the whole season, there's no way any human being could play as well as he did and handle the situation he had better than he did," said Mike Mooney. "It's unbelievable how he did it. Joe's one of the toughest people I've ever been around, mentally as tough as anyone I've ever seen."

"I'm completely different now than when I came to Tech," said Siffri, an All-ACC choice who started the last 26 games of his career, 39 of the final 40. "People who see me now say I'm 100 per cent different. I guess you do a lot of growing up through periods like this, through rough times. And you see the wisdom in people older than you. You start to understand it.

"With my Dad, I realized how important family is—and not just in terms of my immediate family but the Georgia Tech family, how important these people are and how much they helped me get through that situation. I used to think you were evaluated as a football player. Now I realize people here care about you as a person, win or lose.

"A lot of people figure since my Dad died, I'm more depressed. That's not the case. I'm more responsible. I know how to take care of what's going on. I have my priorities in line. Before, they weren't. Coach Ross demands that they are."

chapter 12

Now, it was clear. Now, Georgia Tech would meet Nebraska in the Florida Citrus Bowl, with a genuine chance at a national championship hanging in the balance. Now, Bobby Ross can nearly touch the grail. Never mind that Colorado — despite a loss, a tie and a fifth-down win over Missouri — is still ranked No. 1.

"I'm thinking if we win, we should win the national championship," said Ross. "But I'm not saying that publicly, 'cause I don't want that to be a distraction to the preparation for the game."

Indeed, when the Georgia Tech players returned to campus on December 21 after a pre-Christmas holiday with their families, Ross said, "I've never been a flag-waver. I don't believe in waving a flag for causes you can't do anything about."

By then, much had transpired. Ken Swilling had been named a consensus first-team All-America and was a Thorpe Award finalist as one of the three best defensive backs in the land. Marco Coleman made one All-America first team and joined Swilling, Calvin Tiggle, Willie Clay and Joe Siffri on the All-ACC first team.

And Bobby Ross had been named the winner of the Bobby Dodd Coach of the Year Award, the first Tech coach honored as the nation's best in the award's 15-year history. Ross had also signed a new four-year contract, with a $100,000 base annual salary and considerable perks. "I personally believe that he is the finest football coach in America," Homer Rice said at the time. "It's my hope that Bobby Ross will remain at Tech throughout his coaching career and that he will become another Georgia Tech coaching legend."

By then, the Georgia Tech community had gone Citrus Bowl ballistic. Tech quickly sold its initial allotment of 15,000 tickets, then 8,500 more it requested and received, returning some 4,000 unfilled requests. By game day, there were some 40,000 Tech fans inside the Citrus Bowl. Thousands more couldn't get tickets.

By game day, the Jackets were pumped and primed to play anyone. Not so, however, when they'd returned to campus four days before Christmas. Ross had wrestled with just how to prepare this team for this bowl. Initially after the Georgia victory, Ross considered upcoming exams and how much rest his players needed. Despite extensive bowl experience at Maryland, Ross still wasn't sure how to prepare for the Citrus Bowl.

By the time the Jackets left for Orlando on December 23, the game plan was already completed. Ross had learned from previous bowls to get the game plan in before leaving home. Still, there were other questions to be answered, long before the Jackets left Atlanta.

"Are we gonna take as many as 18 days off?" Ross asked himself. That was the amount of time away from practice he'd given his players: a week after the Georgia game, then exams, then several days at home. Still, Ross wondered, "Is this the right thing to do when you're gonna play the biggest game in the history of your program?"

"In my younger days, I would probably not have done that," Ross said. "But as I looked at it and laid out my practice schedule, I wanted them to be able to prepare for exams, have some time off and go home. So we were able to work it out."

When the players first returned to campus, though, Ross feared he'd blundered terribly. The Jackets were supposed to run on their own at home to maintain some semblance of conditioning. Clearly, many hadn't run enough.

"We came back in terrible shape," said Ralph Friedgen. "We had three or four practices before leaving for Orlando and the kids were dying. I mean, we ran them hard during practices."

And many players, particularly linemen, were gasping for breath. That troubled Ross. But then, he had a far more serious concern.

The Jackets returned to The Flats on Friday, December 21. After practice that day, the team hosted a Christmas party in the school's student union for some 200 children from nearby Techwood Homes. Billy Chubbs dressed up as Santa Claus. Each player escorted a couple of kids to visit Santa Chubbs, then all the children and parents received gifts. It was a warm, touching scene.

Earlier that day, Tom Covington's car had broken down en route to school. After the party, Bobby Ross drove Covington to retrieve his car. It had been stolen, likely by the guy who'd promised Covington he'd watch it while he got help. Then, after taking Covington back to the dorms, Ross returned home to a far greater crisis.

Alice Ross told her husband, "I've got some bad news." His 80-year-old mother, already suffering from Alzheimer's disease aggravated by pneumonia in her lungs, had suffered a severe stroke. Ross immediately called his brother, who said doctors doubted Mrs. Ross would live through the night.

And while he feared and prayed for his mother, Bobby Ross thought, "When is it gonna let up? When is it gonna let up?" After all he and his family and team had endured, now, on the eve of his greatest triumph, his mother lingered near death.

Somehow, Bobby Ross got through it all. Perhaps it was the pain of the most wrenching personal experience. As Alice Ross said, "If you can get through the death of a child, you can get through everything." Alice and Bobby Ross had lost their first child at birth.

Willie Clay lands on the All-ACC first team.

Darryl Jenkins stood tall for four years.

JACK WILKINSON

Surely, Ross's faith helped him through it all. He is a Catholic and devoutly religious in the best sense. His faith is abiding but private, rarely public. Ross doesn't believe in proselytizing. He won't use his celebrity to spread his religious convictions. He attends mass daily, often at the Catholic Student Center on campus. But when he prays, it's in private. And when he says the rosary, as he did often for his mother, it's often while jogging after practice and holding a small, inconspicuous rosary in his hand.

On Saturday, December 22, Bobby Ross had to put his team through two practices while his mind was hundreds of miles away. His mother hung on. She made no progress until three or four days after the Citrus Bowl. By then, her son had gone through yet another emotional wringer.

Understand, Bobby Ross says, "A bowl game is not a good time for a head coach, OK? Assistant coaches don't feel the responsibility for the program until you're a head coach."

As head coach, Bobby Ross was responsible for 132 players in Orlando. All flew to Florida on Sunday the 23rd, Bobby Ross's 54th birthday. At the Orlando airport, the Citrus Bowl reception included a birthday cake for Ross, aglow with 54 candles. Blowing them out, Ross said, "It's great to be 39."

Ross was comfortable enough with his game plan and the players' maturity, and reassured as to their conditioning. So that first night, he gave them a 2 a.m. curfew. The next day, Mrs. Ross suffered a second stroke. And that night, Christmas Eve, Bobby Ross suffered one of the most disheartening moments in his coaching career. And one that could have torn Georgia Tech asunder.

It happened at the most unlikely place: a team Christmas party in a ballroom at the Peabody Hotel, the Jackets' headquarters. It seemed a lovely evening. There were Christmas carolers (accompanied on piano by Coleman Rudolph's mother, Marsha) and Christmas presents for all, all around the room. Ralph Friedgen was supposed to play Santa Claus but the costume was a bit, uh, snug. So his wife Gloria slipped into the Santa suit and into the Santa role, giving out gifts to everyone. Dinner was delicious and the entire evening seemed perfect. So perfect, in fact, that Bobby Ross, who rarely drinks, had asked Kevin Bryant and a few others to join him and his wife in their suite for a champagne Christmas toast.

Ross was the last person to leave the ballroom. Stepping outside, he noticed a group of 35, maybe 40, players, all talking to assistant coach Brian Baker. All talking angrily, particularly Willie Clay and Bobby Rodriguez. They were so upset, at so many things, that Ross immediately asked them all to come back into the ballroom with him and Baker. There, for the next two hours, it all spewed forth, the players venting their anger and airing their grievances.

"The gist of it," said Ross, "was that we were away from home at Christmas and their families weren't there. And ours were."

The families of coaches, administrators and staff were there. But not the players' families. NCAA rules forbid colleges from paying for transportation, room and board for families of athletes. Thus, many Tech parents were unable to travel to the Citrus Bowl prior to Christmas. A few parents, in accordance with NCAA rules, were able to pay $35 each to attend the Christmas Eve dinner but most couldn't afford it. That infuriated some players, who saw coaches and other Tech personnel celebrating Christmas Eve together but who couldn't be with their own parents.

"A lot of guys," said Tom Covington,

"thought, 'What is this dinner for? Is it a dinner for us, or them? The coaches? Everybody just wanted to be with their families."

The players, after all, were young men, mostly 19, 20 and 21 years of age. Most were away from home for Christmas for the first time. And they were homesick. But they were also angry at what many perceived as slights. Some players were offended at the order of presentations that evening. A few players received Christmas gifts, then came the coaches and their wives and children, and administrators and their families. Then came the rest of the players.

"All of the other people were getting recognized before us," said Marco Coleman. "We had a lot of things to tell Coach Ross."

There were season-long gripes: Difficulties in getting new football shoes, more pads, more sweatsuits. Spending money at the Bowl was particularly nettlesome; many Tech players had friends at other schools and had heard rumors about their bowl perks, including rental cars and ample spending money. The Jackets, in accordance with NCAA rules, received about $20 per diem. "It all comes back," said Covington, "to the NCAA and their restrictions."

During the course of the season, in the midst of much hoopla and accomplishment, some players had become disillusioned. Some felt they were being used. "Before, it was always, 'You're doing this for tradition, for Georgia Tech, for your fans,'" said Covington. "When are we doing for ourselves? It's like your sweat and hard work is for what?"

And many black players felt especially isolated. For them, the 12 days of Christmas that Tech spent in Orlando were particularly frustrating—despite an ample, at times non-stop schedule of social events, everything from Sea World to Disney World to MGM Studios tours. "It was hard for the black athletes to go to clubs in that area," said Covington. "They're not our kind of clubs. On International Drive [where the Peabody's located], it's basically discount stores. That doesn't appeal to us. Besides, we didn't have any money, anyway."

As the players talked that night, Bobby Ross listened. And bit his tongue. He was trying, with great difficulty, to sympathize with his players. But he was hurt, deeply hurt, because he was trying to accommodate his players while trying to win a national championship. He gave them a 2 a.m. curfew, in contrast to Nebraska's 10:30 tuck-in. There were several social activities daily for players to choose from. The Citrus Bowl is widely regarded as one of the best bowl trips, and here Ross was trying to further enhance the experience and fun for his players. And here they were, frustrated and angry. That emotionally leveled Bobby Ross.

"I was really disappointed," he says now. "I was really shot down. I was empty."

"Our greatest fear that night was that Coach Ross took it the wrong way," said Covington. "That he felt it was all his fault. It wasn't. We felt it was also the administrators and the NCAA."

"A lot of things came out and Coach Ross gave us his reply," said Coleman. "I respect him for that. A lot of coaches would've said, 'Well, just stay or go.'"

And for awhile, it seemed that's what Bobby Ross was considering: staying or going. Staying on at Tech or going away for good. "For about three or four days," said Ross, "I wasn't sure. At a weaker moment, I might have resigned at the end of the year. I was just really let down."

For several days, Ross didn't even ride the team bus to and from practice, so distraught and disgusted was he. The players and other coaches sensed it, as well as the gravity of the situation. Had those grievances not been aired, Ross admits, there might have been a player rebellion. Having spoken up, though, the players also jeopardized their chances against Nebraska and potentially polarized their head coach.

"A lot of guys were saying, 'If we lose this game, it'll be because of all that,'" said Coleman. "But we sat down and said, 'We should win this for Coach Ross. He listened to us. We want to be treated like men, not boys, and he did that.' "

"If it had not been for that meeting, we'd probably have lost that game," said Ken Swilling. "It was at a time when a lot of frustrations were let out. You need a meeting like that from time to time to get a lot of things off your chest. Maybe that wasn't the opportune time to do it, but the problem arose and people had to vent their frustrations. That was very, very vital for us. It was bound to happen and I'm glad it happened when it did.

"Not being with our families was the

Calvin Tiggle and Georgia Tech over the top.

A force of one: consensus first-team All-American Ken Swilling.

JACK WILKINSON

most upsetting to everyone. It was very sad to me to see the coaches on Christmas Eve with their wives and families. It was like, 'Why can't my family be here?' When they gave the coaches' wives their presents first, that was the point where everybody was like, 'OK, that's it. I'm tired of this, that and the other.' At first, Coach Ross took it as people being upset with him. I don't think that was it at all. Players explained themselves and after that, practice went on as normal, even got better. That meeting was crucial to us winning that game. If you don't have guys like Willie Clay and Bobby Rodriguez giving 100 per cent, you're not gonna win a game like that."

Through it all, Bobby Ross continued to prepare for the biggest game of his life. After practice, he'd return to the hotel, watch practice film alone, set the next day's practice schedule. By then, it was 5 p.m. Ross would take his daily run, shower and change and attend a social event each evening. Somehow, he and his players were able to set aside Christmas Eve and point toward New Year's Day.

"Through it all, we were really able to stay focused, preparation-wise," said Ross. "They weren't gonna let anything interfere with that. I knew two guys were gonna have a helluva game. Shawn and William Bell just had great preparation. I've never seen kids prepare better. By God, if it didn't carry over into the game."

The Jackets sampled the traditional Citrus Bowl social fare, with such outings as Disney World and Sea World. They were transported back to medieval England at Medieval Times. They were extras in a mock filming of "Indiana Jones and the Temple of Doom."

And, of course, there was the annual Squeeze Off, in which three players from each team squeeze as much orange juice as possible. Tom Covington, Jay Martin and Terry Pettis were the Tech squeezers, all wearing Mickey Mouse aprons. The bad news: despite Goofy cheering them on, the Jackets lost to Nebraska, three-fourths of a gallon to a half-gallon of OJ. The good news: no team that's ever won the squeeze off has ever won the bowl game. But then, Nebraska had never played in the Citrus Bowl, and Nebraska was synonymous with bowls.

In the 1980s, Nebraska had the highest winning percentage (83.7) of any school in the land. The Huskers came to Florida with a record of 9–2, extending their NCAA record to 22 straight seasons with at least nine wins. The Citrus Bowl would also be Nebraska's 22nd consecutive bowl game, the last 18 under Tom Osborne. And yet there was considerable grumbling in Lincoln.

The Huskers were once 8–0 and, playing at home in a Big Eight showdown, led Colorado 12–0 after three quarters. But a combination of mistakes, bad breaks, awful weather and desperation led to 27 fourth-quarter Colorado points and a disastrous 27–12 defeat. The Huskers rebounded with a 41–9 thumping of Kansas, but critics sneered that this was simply powerful Nebraska beating up on yet another weakling. Indeed, the Huskers had humiliated a non-league buffet of Baylor, Northern Illinois, Minnesota and Oregon State by a combined 160–21, then feasted on such schedule staples as Kansas State (45–8), Missouri (69–21), Oklahoma State (31–3) and Iowa State (45–13) before falling to Colorado.

Critics charged that Nebraska's offense had become one-sided, as landlocked as its geographic boundaries. That enabled Nebraska to bully most teams, but the lack of a proficient passing attack handcuffed the Huskers against stronger foes. Such criticism was renewed the day after

Thanksgiving, after Nebraska was embarrassed 45–10 at Oklahoma. Just six minutes into the game, quarterback Mickey Joseph was lost for the season when he was tackled late on the sidelines and gashed his leg on the team bench.

That left Osborne with Mike Grant at quarterback and, some felt, no hope in Orlando. Others, though, including some of the Jackets themselves, were still fearful. This was, after all, still Nebraska.

Privately, some Jackets wondered how they'd match up against the Huskers, huge, swift and steeped in tradition. Coleman Rudolph recalled so many friends who'd told him, "You're playing Nebraska? You're playing the powerhouse of the past two decades."

Shawn Jones recalled watching Nebraska on TV so often while growing up. "It's like watching Southern Cal or Notre Dame," Jones said. "Now I have a chance to play them and I want to show them how good we are. They're a great team—speed and tradition—but they wear pants just like we do. We've got all this talent and we've got a chance to show the nation just how good we are.

"It was a once-in-a-lifetime type of thing. I figured we were blessed. Of all Division I-A colleges who could play for a title, we could do it. To go from 2–9 to 7–4 to playing for the title was a blessing."

And Nebraska turned out to be a blessing in disguise. Yes, the Huskers were big, swift and powerful. No, they couldn't throw the ball well and no, they hadn't faced Tech's offensive sophistication. They hadn't seen so many offensive sets, such run-pass balance, so many different types of dropbacks, such complex pass routes. Tech had all of that, practiced it all and employed it brilliantly.

Setting aside its Christmas Eve crisis, Georgia Tech had excellent preparation.

Practices were crisp, players diligent and focused. By New Year's Day, the Jackets were ready to play, having tired of 10 days in Orlando and endless questions about facing powerful, traditional Nebraska.

"The press would ask us all that: 'How are you going to play somebody like Nebraska?' " Kevin Battle said. "Nebraska is just a team like we are. If there's one team I would be literally afraid to play, that would be the San Francisco 49ers."

On New Year's Day, the Yellow Jackets, not the Huskers, were reminiscent of the 49ers.

It was a glorious day in Orlando, the stadium awash in sunshine and glistening with the gold and yellow and white of all those Georgia Tech fans. In pre-game warmups, Nebraska looked physically impressive to everyone, including Bobby Ross. And yet when the Jackets returned to their locker room one last time, Ross told Ralph Friedgen, "Get our receivers into the game quickly, Ralph."

"I could see from the pre-game warmups," said Ross, "that was the one advantage we had."

But then, that was the game plan all along. Nebraska had good speed and quickness up front. Tech would offset that with lots of play-action, counters, bootlegs and all manner of passes. "I just felt that our receivers against their secondary, they couldn't stop us," said Shawn Jones. "I wanted to get the ball upfield to our receivers, then to our backs."

And get the lead. "Since they'd just come off some losses," William Bell said, "we wanted to jump out ahead and make them get down and feel, 'Oh, no, this is going to be one of those days again.' "

Do all that, Bobby Ross felt, and the national championship would take care of itself. His final words to his team in the locker room were, "If we win this game, there's no way they can keep us from being national champions."

"I didn't think he had any reason to lie to us," said Bell. "He said we'd be the only undefeated team in the nation. But regardless of where we end up, we needed to win this game."

"I'm thinking if we win the game, we'll be national champions," said Jim Lavin, who'd turned 22 on Christmas Day in Orlando. "I knew it'd be hard. But I was expecting Notre Dame to beat Colorado."

And Lavin and nearly all his teammates were expecting to beat Nebraska. "Once we got rolling," said Shawn Jones, "it was hard to stop us."

"Once the game started," said Jerimiah McClary, "all the things I grew up thinking about Nebraska were out the window. We just took control."

"I knew that the first series or two, my head was gonna be hurting," said Joe Siffri. "I was going against some big guys. But really, the plays started going exactly like they were supposed to, knocking these guys back. That's when we realized that these were just other players.

"Naturally, when you play Nebraska you're gonna be a little intimidated. You'll be playing their reputation. These guys are from another part of the United States, but we realized they don't grow 'em that much bigger over there or that much better. You realize it's just another team."

On the game's first play—a counter to William Bell—Shawn Jones took the snap and turned for the handoff. And turned the wrong way. "It was all screwed up," Friedgen recalled. Bell still managed to gain eight yards. It was awhile before Jones managed to calm down.

By Friedgen's count, Jones made six errors early in the game, running the wrong plays in certain situations, not

Shawn Jones scrambles on the game's first series.

checking out of others. "He was nervous," said Friedgen. "There was pressure on him. But after the first couple of minutes, Shawn got into the groove."

On that opening possession, on a play-action pass, Jones dropped to his right and found himself in trouble and seemingly trapped in the backfield by Nebraska middle guard Pat Engelbert. "He grabbed my foot," said Jones. "I felt if I could get my foot loose, I could run awhile. They were in man-to-man coverage, with their backs turned to me."

Jones promptly made Pat Engelbert look like Engelbert Humperdink. Jones slipped away, then headed upfield. The Citrus Bowl turf, Jones knew, was rye grass. "Seemed like soil," he said. "You just planted and it was real soft. I saw a guy coming down on me. I tried to split 'em and get as much as I could."

He got 46 yards, turning upfield, then angling left down the sideline. That set up a two-yard touchdown by Stefen Scotton, giving Tech a 7–0 lead.

"I think that set the tone for the day," said Jones. "Everybody was like strangers, feeling each other out. After that, we were real aggressive." Just as Ross, recalling his near-fatal conservatism against Clemson, had vowed Tech would be.

Tech quickly seized the day defensively, too. George O'Leary had seen how quiet his defenders were before the game and wondered if somehow, they weren't ready to play. But then, O'Leary could seldom read his unit's psyche, so quiet as the defense. This day, though, the Jackets were primed from the start for a team averaging 330 yards a game on the ground.

Tech knew that Nebraska's offensive line would take its usual wide splits and run right at the smaller Jackets. "So we just stunted on 'em," said Jerimiah McClary.

After the opening series ended in a

Nebraska punt, McClary and Coleman Rudolph ran off the field and up to O'Leary, shouting, "We can stunt on them all day! They can't stop us!" O'Leary reminded them it was still a bit early; surely Nebraska would adjust.

"The next three series," said McClary, "we did the same thing."

Nebraska went nowhere. Early in the second quarter, O'Leary called upstairs to the coaches' booth and asked, "Have they tightened their splits?" Yes, he was told, Nebraska had tightened up but Tech was still getting penetration.

"So then he just set us free," said McClary, "and started stunting and twisting and everything. We just exploded."

Tech's pass rush turned Nebraska's pocket into Grant's Tomb. Mike Grant could neither pass nor scramble. He misfired on his first four passing attempts and couldn't elude the pass rush. Just 1:55 remained in the first quarter before Nebraska managed a first down. Still, it was just 7–0, Tech self-destructing with fumbles by Jones and Bell (although Tech recovered both) and Scott Sisson's missed field goal attempt after a 45-yard Jones-to-Rodriguez completion.

On Nebraska's first play of the second quarter, though, Coleman Rudolph recovered a Scott Baldwin fumble at the Husker 22. Two plays later, Emmett Merchant made a spectacular catch in the back of the end zone for a 22-yard TD and a 14–0 lead. By now, Tech's confidence was enormous.

Then Jackets scored again. After hitting backup split end Brent Goolsby for 27 yards and Bell for 18 more on a screen, Jones tossed a 2-yard TD to Bell. It was the first of Bell's three touchdowns and gave Georgia Tech a 21–0 lead that stunned even the Jackets themselves.

"We didn't think it was gonna happen that way," said Tom Covington, "so con-

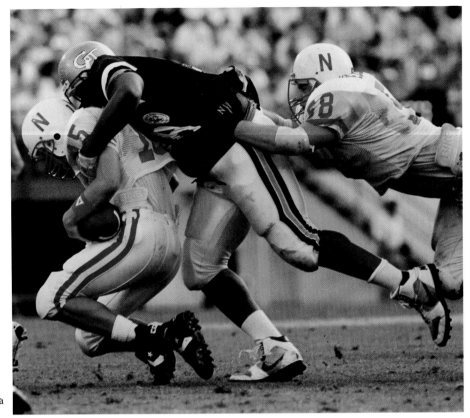

Calvin Tiggle sacks Nebraska quarterback Tom Haasse.

vincing from the start."

It didn't last long. Tom Osborne benched Grant for Tom Haase. He quickly hit freshman tight end Johnny Mitchell for a 30-yard TD behind a badly-beaten Ken Swilling. When newly-inserted I-back Derek Brown burst 50 yards to score, Nebraska trailed by just 21–14.

Tech was forced to punt. Scott Aldredge's kick touched three different Huskers. The ball ricocheted off Nate Turner's right hand, then Tyrone Hughes's shoulder and finally Tyrone Byrd's left hand before disappearing under a pileup. Coming out with the ball was Tech's Jay Martin, who somehow managed to recover and somehow managed to make it to this day.

During his five-year Tech career, Martin established himself as one of the fiercest hitters in the secondary. As a freshman, Mike Mooney recalled watching one Martin tackle that was so ferocious, Mooney wondered if he had the stomach for such a physical level of play. Martin's tenacity came

naturally; his father, Billy, was an All-America tight end at Tech in 1963 who later played five years in the NFL.

His son was nearly as talented, but far less fortunate. Jay Martin played a lot as a freshman in '86, then started at strong safety as a sophomore. But Martin missed the entire '88 season with a back injury, undergoing surgery in February of '89 to repair an injured disk. Then, on November 4th, 1989, Martin tore the anterior cruciate ligament in his right knee against Western Carolina.

As he told Denise Maloof of the *Gwinnett Daily News,* Martin turned to Jay Shoop in the ambulance that day en route to Piedmont Hospital and asked, "To just get it fixed so I could run around in the yard with my kids someday. I was just tired of always having to rehabilitate."

And yet eight months after his second knee surgery and third major operation at Tech, Martin was back for spring practice, back from an injury that usually requires 12

Shawn Jones firing away against the Cornhuskers.

JACK WILKINSON

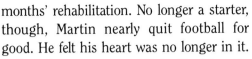

months' rehabilitation. No longer a starter, though, Martin nearly quit football for good. He felt his heart was no longer in it.

But the game was still inside him. So Martin returned and contributed heavily. He started at free safety for the injured Swilling against North Carolina and Duke. He was also a wingback in Tech's goal-line and short-yardage offenses. Now, against Nebraska, Martin recovered the fumble that broke the Huskers' momentum and set up Sisson's 37-yard field goal that gave the Jackets a 24–14 halftime lead and restored their confidence.

In college football, especially in bowl games, all the action isn't always on the field. As the first half ended, Ralph Friedgen and the other Tech assistants in the coaches' box made their way toward the elevator for the trip down to the locker room. Understand that Friedgen is always intense during games, even moreso when the national championship is at stake and momentum seems to be slipping away. As Friedgen headed downstairs, he ran into Citrus Bowl president Chuck Rohe.

"He said, 'Great, great!' " Friedgen recalled. "And I said, 'What do you mean? They just came back.' Chuck said, 'It's great that they came back, Ralph. You're going to win this game, but the TV ratings are back up!' "

Ralph's response: "Screw the ratings!" And off he stormed.

Nebraska threatened again to open the second half. A Husker field goal attempt, though, was blocked by cornerback Keith Holmes. Shawn Jones took immediate advantage. On a crucial third-down play, he found Jerry Gilchrist for 23 yards. After Bell burst 19 yards up the middle, Jones scored from a yard out for a 31–14 lead.

The Huskers, however, still wouldn't concede. At the close of the third quarter, Haase hit another tight end, William Wash-

ington, for a 21-yard TD. Washington, too, had slipped behind Swilling and now Nebraska was back within 31–21.

Georgia Tech then seized control of the fourth quarter, the game, the season and its destiny. The Jackets drove to another score, this one a six-yard run by Bell. With 9:43 left, it was 38–21. Precisely two minutes later, it was a done deal, with Nebraska done in by Bell.

After resting Bell at the start of Tech's next possession, running backs coach Danny Smith reinserted him. On the first play, Bell reasserted himself and assured his team of victory. "I don't even know why I went in," said Bell, who took a handoff, got a great block from Carl Lawson on a blitzing linebacker, and turned in a run for the ages.

Lifting high his legs, Bell stepped through the hole on the right side and then noticed a collision was imminent. "I saw the guy coming, so I kind of lowered my shoulders again to brace myself for the hit," said Bell. "The guy made great contact but I didn't go down. I was trying to roll off him, spin off him. But somehow, we both got turned around and we were back to back. He kept pushing against me, trying to push me back toward the line of scrimmage. There was someone else behind him who sandwiched the first guy between us. I kept trying to roll off him and keep going at the same time because I didn't hear a whistle.

"When I saw that I wasn't making any progress, I just reversed out the other way. The guy who was pressing up against me fell off and so did the guy who helped me sandwich him, and then I was shocked. I took a chance by spinning out because that's usually when the defense is coming over to help. And usually when you spin out like that, you get met and it looks very ugly."

To Tech, it looked breathtakingly beautiful. After spinning left out of that two-man sandwich, Bell angled for the left sideline and raced down it. His mind raced, too: Back to the Duke game, when he'd been caught from behind and kidded mercilessly ever since. To Nebraska, which had such a swift defense, especially linebacker Mike Croel. As he neared the goal line, Bell sensed someone gaining on him. Fearful of being caught from behind twice in one season, Bell dived into the end zone. Then he knelt and said a prayer of thanks.

Never mind that he was in the clear, that no Husker could have caught him. Bell dived anyway, for safety's sake, not style points. The Citrus Bowl erupted again. Now Tech's triumph was assured. Now, despite the scoreboard matrix that flashed, "Georgia Tech 1990 National Champions," the waiting began.

William Bell finished with 126 yards rushing and three TDs. Defensively, Tech had held Nebraska to 127 yards rushing, 204 below its average. But the true MVP of Georgia Tech's 45–21 victory was Shawn Jones. He completed 16 of 23 passes for 277 yards and two touchdowns. He rushed for 41 more yards and another TD. He set career highs for passing yardage and total offense (318 yards). He riddled Nebraska for more points than any bowl opponent in Husker history.

For the season, Shawn Jones set a Georgia Tech total offense record with 2,285 yards, passing for 2,008 yards and 13 TDs. He directed the second most prolific offense in Georgia Tech history. For the season, the Jackets scored 379 points, the fourth-highest total in school history and the most points in 72 years.

With that, the Jackets finished 11–0–1. But would they finish No. 1? Opinions varied.

Ralph Friedgen: "When we beat Nebraska, I didn't see where it was even close. I had seen Colorado on film. When

Keith Holmes gets up to block Nebraska field goal try.

you compare scores, Illinois beat Colorado and Clemson crushes Illinois. Nebraska's beating Colorado 12–0 going into the fourth quarter. If comparative scores are the only way to do it, that and the fact that we're undefeated should make us No. 1."

Mike Mooney: "As soon as the game was

JACK WILKINSON

over, we all had this feeling. We were national champs but we'd worked for four years to get to this point and now somehow, they're gonna take it away from us. The day before the Citrus Bowl, Coach Ross told us, 'Don't worry about if Notre Dame beats Colorado. If you win, you're gonna win the national championship.' I thought, 'Come on.' We should be, but will we?"

Marco Coleman: "If Colorado won, I knew they were gonna be No. 1. But we deserved it. We didn't lose any games. We had a tougher schedule. No one laid down. We got no fifth downs."

Tom Covington: "After the game, a lot of Nebraska players told us, 'You guys deserve the title.' Still, you know a lot of people are skeptical of you. It all depends on opinions."

Bobby Ross: "I felt we deserved it. We beat a good Nebraska team and we were the only undefeated team in the country. What else could we do?"

Tech could only wait, and hope.

Shortly after the Citrus Bowl, thousands of Tech fans and many players went to the Church Street Station bar, restaurant and entertainment complex in downtown

William Bell scoring his third TD of the game.

Jubilant fans tearing down the goalposts.

Orlando for the traditional post-game Boola Bowl. Some fans carried remnants of the goal posts. They came to see the official presentation of the Citrus Bowl winner's trophy. Accepting was Bobby Ross.

In the summer of '87, Ross had come to Church Street Station to address the local Georgia Tech alumni group. That time, Ross was dismayed by the meager turnout and obvious lack of enthusiasm, telling Kevin Bryant, "Well, they just don't care. Like most Tech people, they don't care."

But now, having hopped in a limousine with Shawn Jones, Thomas Balkcom, and Homer and Phyllis Rice, Ross returned to Church Street Station in triumph. The limo pulled up to the exact same spot at which Ross had arrived 3½ years earlier. This time, the thousands of Tech fans made it impossible for Ross to pass, so he had to be taken inside through the back door. For Kevin Bryant, the irony was as rich as the moment.

"The exact same spot," Bryant said. "Here we are carrying the trophy and I thought, 'This is really ironic. Three years later, we have to bring Bobby in the back door through the kitchen to get him to the platform.' "

Ross didn't linger long, though. He returned to the Peabody, packed some clothes and went to the airport. There, a private jet was waiting for him, to fly him to Virginia to finally see his mother. Ross took a cab from the airport and arrived at his father's home just as Rocket Ismail was returning the punt. When Buss Ross told him what had just happened, Bobby Ross merely shrugged, then drove to the hospital to see his mother.

"I didn't lose anything over that," said Ross. "Too many other things on my mind."

In Orlando, though, the Tech reaction was far more animated, and anguished.

Nearly all of the Tech players, coaches and staff watched the Orange Bowl back at the Peabody Hotel. Forget the famed Peabody ducks. The Fighting Irish were foremost in Tech's mind. Some Tech players, family, friends and staff watched the Notre Dame-Colorado game in a banquet room reserved for Tech. Most players, though, watched the Orange Bowl up in their rooms, while some Tech coaches and assistants watched in the hotel lobby bar.

For more than 55 minutes, Notre Dame labored offensively and Georgia Tech groaned. "Here's Notre Dame, they're supposed to have the best talent in the world, and they didn't throw the ball worth a darn," said Friedgen, watching in the hospitality room.

But the Irish were still playing with the Rocket. In the waning minutes, Rocket Ismail nearly wrote the perfect ending to the Georgia Tech story. Fielding a Colorado punt, Ismail weaved his way through the Buffaloes and scored an apparent winning touchdown. A touchdown that would undoubtedly give Georgia Tech the national championship.

Down in the lobby bar sat George O'Leary and his brother, Pete. Another

Tech players, watching in their hotel room, can't believe Rocket's TD is called back.

brother, Tom, was riding the elevator as Ismail returned the punt. The hotel shook so mightily, it rocked the elevator, leaving Tom O'Leary as shaken as the elevator itself. "What happened?" he asked when he got off in the lobby.

Thomas Balkcom knew. He was watching the game in T.J. Edwards' room, along with Jerimiah McClary, Ken Swilling, Darryl Swilling, Jason McGill, Damon Wilson and several young ladies. When Ismail scored, the room — like the rest of the hotel — went wild. In the ensuing celebration, someone inadvertently turned off the TV. When it came back on, the Jackets stared and shrieked in horror as the camera focused on the penalty flag.

Notre Dame had been called for clipping, the punt return called back. Notre Dame was doomed and so, too, it seemed, were Tech's national championship hopes, so cruelly dashed. Up in their rooms and down in the lobby, the Jackets were beside themselves. Even Tech basketball coach Bobby Cremins stalked the lobby, lamenting, "That was our national championship, right there."

Some, but not many, Jackets held out some slight hope. "Colorado deserved to lose for kicking it to the Rocket," said Marco Coleman. "I think we're No. 1. Besides, I didn't think it was a clip. Notre Dame got the bad end of the stick."

"I still thought, somehow, we'd have to be No. 1," said Jim Lavin. "If there was a Santa Claus, then we would be No. 1."

Alas, Santa doesn't have a vote in the AP poll and Colorado already had a comfortable lead among the AP's sportswriters, if a more tenuous hold among UPI's coaches. And then there was the genetics factor: at LSU, Lavin's father's senior season was 1957, just missing out on LSU's national championship in 1958. "After I watched the Colorado game," Lavin said, "I thought, 'This is gonna happen to me, too.'"

Tom Covington was still hopeful, reasoning, "Well, look at Colorado. They didn't beat Notre Dame. Notre Dame lost it."

No matter. Colorado had precedent and prejudice on its side. No No. 1 team that won a bowl game had ever been bumped from the top spot. And many sportswriters held an anti-ACC bias (calling it a basketball conference that happened to play football). They also questioned Tech's schedule and credentials. All those factors were obvious on January 2, when the Jackets returned to Atlanta and their fears were confirmed.

"Bummer!" read the front-page headline in that afternoon's *Atlanta Journal*. Although Tech closed the gap slightly, the Jackets were still a decided second to Colorado. "It was such a terrible feeling," recalled Tom Covington. "On the plane ride home, you felt the season was for naught."

"It was almost like we had gone undefeated for nothing," said Ken Swilling. "For no respect at all."

"Our only hope then was the coaches," said Mike Mooney. "Honestly, I didn't think we'd get it. I knew it'd be closer than AP, but I didn't think we'd get it."

After the final AP poll was announced, Tech sports information director Mike Finn asked George O'Leary and Ralph Friedgen to fill in for Bobby Ross at a press conference. There, they both expressed their disappointment.

At the press conference, Atlanta sportscaster Randy Waters of WXIA-TV asked Friedgen if he'd come down to the station that evening and do a live interview once the UPI vote was announced. Friedgen agreed and drove home with his family. By then, most Tech players and coaches were resigned to their fate. Soon, things started getting quite interesting in Mike Finn's office and became nearly as dramatic as the closing seconds of the Virginia game.

The first phone call from a UPI staffer came about 4 o'clock. Finn couldn't believe his ears. Incredibly, with four votes still outstanding, Tech was in the lead. But it was too close to call.

About 10 minutes later, the phone rang again. UPI, again. "With two votes out, you're still in the lead," Finn was told. "But it's too close to call."

Another 10 minutes, another update. "There's one vote out. It's tied."

And finally, the tie-breaker: "You guys won. By one vote."

With that, they all started screaming, Finn and his assistants Frank Zang, Mike Stamus and Allison George. Earlier that day, Finn had called Bobby Ross with the AP results. Now he again called Bus Ross, who said his son had already left Williamsburg for the Richmond airport. Finn called the Delta counter at the airport and left word for Ross to call him. It was urgent.

Meanwhile, all around Atlanta, the Jackets learned of their great fortune in a variety of ways.

Ralph Friedgen and his family were driving south on I-75, heading for the Channel 11 studios and listening to WCNN on the radio. He heard the announcer, speaking in a monotone, say that Georgia Tech had won the UPI national championship by one vote.

"What did he say?!" Friedgen asked his wife.

"I think he said we won," Gloria Friedgen said with some trepidation.

"What was the other part?" her husband asked.

"It was like a blur," said Friedgen. "Then he came back on and said that the coaches had voted and Georgia Tech had won by one vote."

Friedgen started screaming and promptly drove right off the highway. He quickly regained control of his car—if not his composure — and got back on I-75,

rushing toward the TV station. "That's kinda how I wanted to end up," said Friedgen, who got to the station in time.

Mike Mooney, Jim Gallagher and backup kicker Alan Waters were at Waters's apartment when they turned on the telephone answering machine and heard Darryl Jenkins' cry: "Mike! Alan! We won the national championship in UPI by one vote!"

Mooney immediately dialed Mark Hutto's dorm room. The line was busy. So Mooney called Jenkins and warned, "Darryl, if you're lying to me, I'm gonna kill you!"

Jenkins reassured him. "And we jumped around like two-year-olds," said Mooney. They turned on the TV and saw Joe Siffri. Again. A TV crew from WAGA had already come to Siffri's house to film a live, if somber, interview. Afterwards, after going off the air, the crew was packing up its equipment in a van when one crew member told Siffri, "Hold on a minute! We need to get you back on the air!"

Siffri suspected nothing. Perhaps WAGA needed to fill some air time. "What's that?" he heard the crewman say, talking with the studio, then talking to him: "It just turned out that UPI picked y'all No. 1." Within minutes, Siffri was back on the air.

"Now my face is glowing," said Siffri. "My whole perspective had changed."

Tom Covington saw Siffri's face while he was watching TV at a friend's house in Lithonia. "I about jumped through the roof," Covington said. "Just went crazy. Thank God, somebody actually gave us what we deserved. Somebody actually saw the light, that one vote."

Ken Swilling thought he was dreaming. Half-asleep in his dorm room, with the TV set on, he heard something about Tech and No. 1. Startled, he jumped up and said, "No. 1?" Indeed. Swilling immediately called his mother, who shared in his joy.

"It was very nice to have someone

Darryl Jenkins hoists Citrus Bowl trophy.

respect us," said Swilling. "I thought that was the most important thing about winning the UPI coaches' poll."

In his dorm room, Shawn Jones got a congratulatory phone call just as the story was being aired on TV. "I felt good," Jones said. "I felt relieved. I felt that justice was done."

Bobby Ross finally found out that evening, sitting in the Richmond airport, waiting for his flight to Atlanta. Alice Ross called her husband there and told him to call Mike Finn immediately. "What is it?" he asked.

"I think," said Mrs. Ross, "that UPI voted you No. 1."

"Well, hallelujah!" shouted Bobby Ross. Absolutely thrilled, he called Mike Finn. Then Ross bummed an early ride home aboard an empty Delta charter that was returning to Atlanta. The plane had just returned from New Orleans and dropped off hundreds of disappointed Virginia fans who watched the Wahoos lose to Tennessee in the final minute of the Sugar Bowl. Back at Hartsfield, Ross held an impromptu news conference before returning home.

Now, he recalls the entire scenario and calls it "the most freakish series of events that could ever happen. Almost like, 'How could these things happen?'"

But they did, and Ross was thankful and overjoyed. "I was really excited," he said. "I didn't think I'd be that excited. But I got a taste of it. The thrill of being the No. 1 football team in the country really got to me."

When Ross got the first call from Mike Finn at the hospital in Virginia, informing him Colorado had won the AP title, he was deeply disappointed and hardly optimistic about his chances with UPI. "I figured if one wasn't gonna vote us, the other wasn't," said Ross. "I'll tell you what happened. A lot of coaches watched us play and

I think they voted for us. At the coaches convention [the annual American Football Coaches Association, held in New Orleans in early January], a lot of coaches told me, 'Y'all were pretty good.' Like they were really surprised.

"I think the way we won it was nice," said Bobby Ross. "And I don't mind sharing it."

For that, numerous people have taken credit. One of Tech secondary coach Chuck Priefer's best friends is an assistant at Illinois, who always votes for Illini coach John Mackovic in the UPI poll. Naturally, he called Priefer and claimed credit for Tech's title. And then there was the phone call Mike Finn got from a sports information director somewhere in the Southwest. Seems the head coach at that school wanted to vote Colorado No. 1. Then the SID reminded him that Georgia Tech was undefeated.

"You're right," said the coach. "Let's make them No. 1."

No. 1 by one vote. "How many stories," Finn wondered, "must there have been like that to make us No. 1?" Who knows? Who cares?

In addition to UPI, Georgia Tech was also named national champion by *The Sporting News* and Scripps Howard News Service. Bobby Ross was the runaway consensus coach of the year, winning nine different national coach of the year awards. One of the most meaningful was the Bobby Dodd Award, presented at the Atlanta Hilton on Feburary 26. Having gone through so much at Georgia Tech, having lost a granddaughter, his parents' ill health and then a son fighting in the Persian Gulf War, Ross was emotionally overcome when accepting the award named for the coach he so admired.

By then, Ross and the Jackets had already savored a city's embrace. The Mon-

1952 team holds congratulatory banner.

day after the Citrus Bowl, Atlanta threw a joyous tickertape parade for the Yellow Jackets. Thousands upon thousands of Atlantans turned out to express their appreciation and affection for the Jackets. Ross nearly fell asleep during the parade in one car in the motorcade, so sick was he with flu and working on little sleep.

Yet Ross recovered to attend the coaches' convention in New Orleans. He also took an overnight detour, flying to Cleveland in Art Modell's private Lear jet to talk with the Cleveland Browns' owner about his coaching vacancy. Ross was first contacted about the job while visiting his mother in Virginia. He felt he owed it to his family, and himself, to at least meet with Modell. Had Ross wanted it, the job was his. Instead, he decided to remain at Tech.

"I had an inner feeling he wouldn't leave," said Homer Rice. "I knew what was going on. I knew Bobby was highly coveted and will continue to be. But something told me he would not leave this team."

He didn't. Ross returned to New Orleans, returned home, then returned to what he knows and does best: working. He hit the recruiting trail hard until the February 8 signing date and helped Tech sign some exceptional prospects.

As for Georgia Tech's immediate prospects, Ross is rather optimistic. With 14 starters returning, Tech was ranked as high

as No. 4 in the pre-season and hopes to extend its 16-game unbeaten streak. It won't be easy. Tech must rebuild its offensive line, and quickly; the Jackets were chosen to face Penn State in the season-opening Kickoff Classic in East Rutherford, N.J.

But Shawn Jones returns as a legitimate Heisman Trophy candidate. So does Ken Swilling, who opted not to turn pro and should benefit from a switch to strong safety and a healthy foot. And defensively, Ross says, "If we play the way I think we can, this could be the finest defense I've ever coached."

Whatever unfolds, Ross will always have that championship season of 1990. But then, Georgia Tech's title was not merely a national championship but a real triumph — a triumph of an indomitable spirit, a triumph over odds and tragedies, a triumph worthy of high praise. Indeed, Bobby Ross and the Yellow Jackets did something truly noble. In winning a national championship, they also restored a once-lustrous tradition and made it shimmer anew. That is far more difficult than merely winning a championship, or defending one.

And what exactly does winning a national championship mean? Different things to different people. Listen:

Willie Clay: "When I look back on things,

Mayor Jackson at post-parade rally with Ross, Jenkins, President Crecine, and McClary.

Ross, with Alice Dodd, receiving the Bobby Dodd Coach of the Year Award.

One happy Jerrelle Williams.

it's just like a dream, something that went on and I was a part of. I can always say I played a big part in getting Georgia Tech football back on the map. And I played for a national championship team. A lot of people can't say that. Regardless of what happens, I will always remember these guys, this special team. Hopefully, we'll be back for a sequel and go and win it again, but I don't think it will mean as much to me as this year. Because it was the first time. It's

something I will always cherish."

Ralph Friedgen: "It was one of those things that worked out and everything fell into place—as much as nothing worked for the first two years. Maybe it was justified that this should work, just this once. I told my wife, 'You know, very few people achieve their life goals.' It's a great feeling. Many people don't understand guys like myself, who are career coaches. I wouldn't know what to do if I got out of coaching. And then to have this chance. Still, I don't think our kids really understand what they've accomplished. And I'm not sure many people around here understand, either. People said you could never win a national championship here because of academics and everything else. But we showed them you can, and you can do it right. You don't have to cheat and you don't have to get every blue-chip guy in America. You can have all these bricks that are great players, but if you don't have any cement to put in there, those bricks aren't real sturdy. The important thing is how all these kids work together, and then you have to blend them all together. That's what makes it all rewarding."

Shawn Jones: "It means a lot. When I did it, I was 21 years old. I don't even know if Joe Montana won a national championship. It's like you could stick your hand in a hat of 1,000 names and pull your name out. I just happened to be that one, we just happened to be that team. It was just a blessing."

Tom Covington: "It's a whole new world. Now it's, like, 'Here's the Georgia Tech football team.' It all comes down to respect. It's not arrogance but you like to be respected. You're one of the elite. It's relaxing, too. You know they're not gonna be snickering behind your back any more. It's nice to always have people smiling at you. Just to win, and also know you have the potential to do it again, it's a whole new feeling."

Jim Lavin: "We went undefeated, won the ACC championship and the national championship, and we'll always be remembered as one of the best teams ever on this campus."

Kevin Battle: "It's a great joy and relief. Every day in practice, you work hard. And if you lose a lot, you say, 'What's the use of practicing?' Now that you're national champions, all this pays off. It's a great

feeling. I remember walking into a mall and I didn't see nothing but Georgia Bulldogs and University of Miami sweatshirts and hats, and I walked in and said, 'Excuse me, do you have a Tech sweatshirt?' They said, 'A what? Oh yeah, way in the corner.' I walked in the back and picked the dust and spider webs off the shirt. Now that we're No. 1, I walk into the mall and get bombarded by Tech. Tech is everywhere. I walk in now and ask for a Tech hat and it's, 'Oh, man, I just sold the last one but I've got more on order.' It's great, I can hold my head up high. Now, I not only go to a great institution of higher learning but also a great school that's No. 1 in the nation. A lot of people are now coming out of the closet. I call them out-of-the-closet Tech fans. I like that. They don't have to be wishy-washy about it. They now say, 'Yeah, I like Tech, I've been a Tech fan since I was this high.' I say, 'Oh, really?' It's a good feeling not to get laughed at any more."

Mike Mooney: "There was a closeness on our team that was so apparent. I never could see the defense play, I was always on the bench. When I watched the Virginia game on tape, those guys were out there together doing whatever it took. And when Tiggle knocked that pass down in the end zone, there must have been six guys — before he even hit the ground — jumping on him, slapping him on the back. Coaches can't teach that and you can't fake it. I think that was unique and probably why we were the best team in the country. I'm so glad I came to Tech. For awhile, I thought I'd made the wrong decision. But I'm close to graduating, won a national championship and met a lot of good people. I'll be able to get a good job, too. I think it's all gonna mean more to me in a couple of years. I know it means more to me knowing how to lose, going 2–9, 3–8. And I know in nine years, I'm gonna say, 'Damn! That's awesome! and I was part of that.' "

Ken Swilling: "When I first got here, it was, like, 'Georgia Tech football? What's that?' You'd say, 'You coming to see us play?' and it was, 'Why? You're gonna lose anyway.' Coming home from the Virginia game was a sign of acceptance for me. Even knowing we had just won a big game, that's when I knew we had been accepted here as a football team and people. Even today, people, regular students, come up and talk to you. It seemed like there used to be a wall between the regular students and athletes, especially football players. Now that wall is coming down. It's very open and we have a chance to associate with the regular students. They treat us no different than anybody else and I really enjoy that. Where I come from, Toccoa, it's a small town, everybody knows everybody and it's just common nature to speak to everybody. When I came here, it was, like, 'Why isn't anybody speaking to me?' It was very awkward. Most times when you speak to somebody, you expect them to speak back. Now that's changing here. They're speaking back to you."

Homer Rice: "This is the ultimate for me. Football is my sport. To win a national championship and have your coach win every coach of the year award out there is a dream that comes true. This is where I'd want all our sports to be, at this level, but particularly football. It's my sport and that makes me extremely happy."

Joe Siffri: "To me, it's not a national championship team, just a bunch of guys I've been hanging out with for four, five years. That's why I don't understand why people make such a big deal out of seeing me. 'Hey, you're Joe Siffri!' Wait a minute. I'm just me. It used to be if you said you were a Georgia Tech engineer, you got more respect than if you were a Georgia Tech football player. People probably would rather not have been seen with a football player. Now we're like heroes. You have kids who say they're you and wanna wear your jerseys. We've got footballs coming into the football office like crazy to be autographed. A lot of people say, 'You were so bad before, how can you explain being national champions?' Coach Ross made us go through the tough times and do things the right way in order to get to that point. And learning how to grow up and depend on people and work for someone else and not just for the benefits for yourself. To actually be on the field and not be upset when you miss a block because you're gonna get yelled at by a coach but because you let down your buddy. That became a crucial part of our success and I learned how important that is. I have no interest in the NFL, in playing football anymore. But I wouldn't mind playing for Tech again. I was watching the Virginia game a few weeks ago. I don't wanna play pro ball. I wanna play for Tech again."

Thomas Balkcom: "When I think about it sometimes, I still can't believe it. You know all the work you put into it. I have to be careful sometimes. I get excited. I start sweating just thinking about it again. People say ghosts hang around stadiums and all that. I'm part of that. I'm part of history. Sometimes, I'll be working out in the stadium with Calvin and Jerimiah and Chris Simmons and Stefen and I'll say, 'Man, can you hear it?' Calvin'll say, 'What's that?' 'The crowd!' I'll say. 'Yeah, I can hear it. We did it this year, fellas.' Winning it all was wonderful. You'll always remember everything you were doing, all the guys. It'll always be something bright, no matter how you're doing. I'll always remember that at this time in my life, no matter how down and out I am, I was the best. I was a champion. No one can ever take that away from you. Your son or your daughter can look up to you and say, 'My Dad was the best.' "

Joe Siffri stayed and became a champion.

The 1990 UPI National Championship Trophy.

FINAL STATISTICS

1990 RECORD: 11-0-1 Overall, 6-0-1 ACC (1st)

National Champions—UPI, Scripps Howard, The Sporting News

TOTAL OFFENSE

Player	G	Play	Rush	Pass	Total	Avg
Jones	11	336	277	2008	2285	207.7
Howard	5	15	-9	28	19	3.8
(All others same as rushing)						
TECH	**11**	**779**	**2298**	**2036**	**4334**	**394.0**
Opponents	**11**	**743**	**1220**	**2022**	**3242**	**294.7**

RUSHING

	G	Att	Yds	PAvg	GAvg	TD	LP
Bell	10	161	891	5.5	89.1	5	52
Wright	10	89	395	4.4	39.5	4	21
Jones	11	91	277	3.0	25.2	6	36
Scotton	11	71	261	3.7	23.7	5	18
Edwards	5	58	248	4.3	49.6	1	25
Lawson	11	25	90	3.6	8.2	1	10
Rodriguez	11	2	53	26.5	4.8	1	35
Tisdel	7	6	29	4.8	4.1	0	13
Reese	10	5	23	4.6	2.3	0	8
Hamilton	4	6	21	3.5	5.3	0	5
Bowman	2	2	11	5.5	5.5	0	7
Gilchrist	10	2	8	4.0	0.8	1	12
Lester	11	1	0	0.0	0.0	0	0
Howard	5	5	-9	—	—	0	0
TECH	**11**	**524**	**2298**	**4.4**	**208.9**	**24**	**52**
Opponents	**11**	**434**	**1220**	**2.8**	**110.9**	**7**	**26**

PASSING

	Att	Comp	Int	Pct	Yds	Avg	TD
Jones	245	142	12	.580	2008	182.6	13
Howard	10	4	1	.400	28	5.6	1
TECH	**255**	**146**	**13**	**.573**	**2036**	**185.1**	**14**
Opponents	**309**	**151**	**24**	**.489**	**2022**	**183.8**	**5**

RECEIVING

	G	Rec	Yds	Avg	RPG	TD	LP
Merchant	11	29	489	16.9	2.6	3	27
Rodriguez	11	27	493	18.3	2.5	3	54
Lester	11	16	236	14.8	1.5	3	40
Covington	11	15	175	11.7	1.4	0	38
Gilchrist	10	13	162	12.5	1.3	1	43
Bell	10	13	159	12.2	1.3	2	78
Scotton	11	9	71	7.9	0.8	0	14
Edwards	5	5	81	16.2	1.0	0	46
Goolsby	11	4	42	10.5	0.4	0	17
Wright	10	4	12	3.0	0.4	0	8
Pettis	6	3	38	12.7	0.5	0	25
McGill	9	2	26	13.0	0.2	0	14
Rice	11	2	19	9.5	0.2	0	11
Walker	8	1	10	10.0	0.1	0	10
Goshay	11	1	8	8.0	0.1	1	8
Lawson	11	1	8	8.0	0.1	0	8
MacKendree	7	1	7	7.0	0.2	1	7
TECH	**11**	**146**	**2036**	**13.9**	**13.3**	**14**	**78**
Opponents	**11**	**151**	**2022**	**13.4**	**13.7**	**5**	**69**

INTERCEPTIONS

	G	Int	Yds	Avg	TD	LP
K.Swilling	9	5	34	6.8	0	22
Clay	11	3	82	27.3	0	42
Day	10	2	18	9.0	0	18
Fry	11	2	8	4.0	0	8
Holmes	10	2	0	0.0	0	0
Ms. Coleman	3	2	0	0.0	0	0
Mi. Williams	10	1	83	83.0	1	83
Tiggle	11	1	38	38.0	0	38
Bellamy	11	1	34	34.0	0	34
Ma. Williams	11	1	4	4.0	0	4
Weaver	11	1	4	4.0	0	4
J. Williams	11	1	1	1.0	0	1
Balkcom	11	1	1	1.0	0	1
Peoples	11	1	0	0.0	0	0
TECH	**11**	**24**	**307**	**12.8**	**1**	**83**
Opponents	**11**	**13**	**171**	**13.2**	**0**	**40**

SCORING

			PAT			
Player	TD	2PAT	DPAT	KPAT	FG	Pts
Sisson	—	—	—	39-39	15-23	84
Bell	7	—	—	—	—	42
Jones	6	1-1	—	—	—	38
Scotton	5	—	—	—	—	30
Wright	4	—	—	—	—	24
Rodriguez	4	—	—	—	—	24
Lester	3	1-1	—	—	—	20
Merchant	3	—	—	—	—	18
Gilchrist	2	—	—	—	—	12
Goshay	1	—	—	—	—	6
Edwards	1	—	—	—	—	6
Lawson	1	—	—	—	—	6
Tisdel	1	—	—	—	—	6
Mi. Williams	1	—	—	—	—	6
Lavin	1	—	—	—	—	6
MacKendree	1	—	—	—	—	6
TECH	**41**	**2-2**	**0-0**	**39-39**	**15-23**	**334**
Opponents	**13**	**3-4**	**0-0**	**9-9**	**24-28**	**165**

SCORING BY QUARTERS

	1st	2nd	3rd	4th	Total	Avg
TECH	69	115	98	97	*379	31.6
Opponents	34	68	44	40	*186	15.5

*Florida Citrus Bowl included. Other bowl stats do not count in season totals.

PUNTING

	G	No	Yds	Blk	Avg	Net	LP
Aldredge	11	53	1942	0	36.6	33.6	54
TECH	**11**	**53**	**1942**	**0**	**36.6**	**33.6**	**54**
Opponents	**11**	**65**	**2464**	**1**	**37.9**	**34.2**	**56**

KICKOFF RETURNS

	G	No	Yds	Avg	TD	LP
Tisdel	7	18	531	29.5	1	87
K. Swilling	9	2	44	22.0	0	31
McGill	9	9	195	21.7	0	36
Wright	10	4	76	19.0	0	52
Martin	11	2	20	10.0	0	17
Rush	11	3	28	9.3	0	13
Weaver	11	1	6	6.0	0	6
TECH	**11**	**39**	**900**	**23.1**	**1**	**87**
Opponents	**11**	**54**	**1044**	**19.3**	**0**	**35**

PUNT RETURNS

	G	No	Yds	Avg	TD	LP
McGill	9	27	163	6.0	0	20
Clay	11	14	82	5.9	0	26
Lester	11	1	-1	—	0	-1
TECH	**11**	**42**	**244**	**5.8**	**0**	**26**
Opponents	**11**	**20**	**155**	**7.8**	**0**	**17**

MISCELLANEOUS YARDAGE (FGs blocked & fumbles advanced)

Player	G	No	Yds	Avg	TD	LP
J. Williams	11	1	31	31.0	0	31
Day	10	1	11	11.0	0	11
Lavin	11	1	0	0.0	0	0
TECH	**11**	**3**	**42**	**14.0**	**0**	**31**
Opponents	**11**	**1**	**11**	**11.0**	**0**	**11**

TEAM STATISTICS

	Tech	Opponents
Total First Downs	231	174
First Downs Rushing	122	81
First Downs Passing	97	83
First Downs Penalties	12	10
Fumbles-Lost	28-13	22-16
Number of Penalties-Yards	54-397	59-442
Quarterback Sacks By-Yards	45-239	11-85
Third Down Conversions	61-151	50-162
Third Down Conversion Pct.	.404	.309
Fourth Down Conversions	5-9	4-13
Average Time of Possession	31:39	28:21

FINAL STATISTICS

DEFENSE

Player, Pos.	Solo	Pri	Ast	Total	For Loss	QB Sack	Fumble Caused	Fumble Recd	Pass Int	Pass BrUp	Press Pass
J. Williams, ILB	25	55	65	145	2-4	5-30	3	3	1	2	3
Tiggle, ILB	24	51	59	134	3-3	3-9	2	2	1	7	3
Mo. Coleman, OLB	24	24	33	81	6-17	13-59	1	--	--	--	19
K. Swilling, FS	19	16	36	71	1-1	1-3	2	--	5	5	2
Rudolph, DT	11	26	29	66	7-28	5-31	--	1	--	--	10
McClary, DT	10	24	23	57	4-5	1-4	--	--	--	--	5
Battle, NG	7	28	21	56	2-6	4-12	1	1	--	--	4
Day, CB	16	18	22	56	2-2	--	--	--	2	10	1
Fry, ILB	12	21	23	56	2-10	2-11	--	--	2	6	4
Balkcom, SS	11	15	29	55	3-16	1-10	--	--	1	1	4
Clay, CB	16	15	24	55	2-4	--	--	2	3	14	--
Simmons, OLB	7	15	23	45	1-2	4-17	1	2	--	--	13
Ma. Williams, OLB	12	17	15	44	3-5	5-30	1	1	1	3	3
Martin, SS	6	11	25	42	1-3	--	--	--	--	3	1
Holmes, CB	7	8	20	35	1-5	--	--	1	2	4	2
Peoples, SS	6	9	19	34	--	--	--	--	1	1	--
Johnson, OLB	7	13	3	23	--	2-15	--	1	--	--	2
Scott, CB	3	5	8	16	--	--	--	--	--	--	--
Pharr, ILB	3	5	7	15	--	--	--	1	--	1	--
D. Swilling, ILB	3	6	5	14	1-3	--	--	--	--	--	1
Bellamy, FS	5	2	6	13	--	--	--	--	1	1	--
Travis, ILB	1	3	8	12	--	--	1	--	--	1	--
Goshay, TE	2	6	2	10	--	--	--	--	--	--	--
Waters, K	2	4	3	9	--	--	--	--	--	--	--
Weaver, OLB	3	0	5	8	--	--	--	--	1	--	--
Ms. Coleman, CB	2	2	2	6	--	1-13	--	--	2	--	--
Rice, TE	3	1	2	6	--	--	--	--	--	--	--
Baxter, NG	1	2	2	5	1-2	--	--	--	--	--	2
Rush, CB	3	1	1	5	--	--	--	--	--	--	--
Parker, C	3	0	2	5	--	--	--	--	--	--	--
Kimsey, DT	0	3	2	5	--	--	--	--	--	--	--
Mi. Williams, CB	3	1	0	4	--	--	--	--	1	1	--
Ray, CB	0	2	2	4	--	--	--	--	--	1	--
Cox, OLB	2	0	1	3	--	1-9	--	--	--	--	--
Harris, FB	0	1	0	1	--	--	--	--	--	--	--
Reese, FB	0	0	1	1	--	--	--	--	--	--	--
Gallagher	0	0	1	1	--	--	--	--	--	--	--
Siffri, G	0	0	0	0	--	--	--	1	--	--	--
Lester, WR	0	0	0	0	--	--	1	--	--	--	--
TOTALS	259	410	529	1198	41-113	*45-245	15	16	24	61	79

* Where more than one player was involved in a sack, each individual was credited with a full sack

FIELD GOALS ATTEMPTED (Underline indicates FG made) Scott Sisson: 42NCS, 39NCS, 20UTC, 32UTC, 33UTC, 20SC, 42SC, 29MD, 48MD, 50CL, 37NC, 20NC, 27NC, 33DU, 57DU, 43DU, 32VA, 37VA, 32VT, 34VT, 33VT, 38VT, 22GA

	Score	First Downs	Yards Rush	Yards Pass	Passes Att/Cmp	Had Int	Fumbles No/Lost	Penalties No/Yds	Att
N.C. State	13	11	104	113	18/11	2	3/3	4/30	40,021
GEORGIA TECH	21	16	145	123	19/9	1	4/3	1/6	Home
UT-Chattanooga	9	14	126	122	21/7	5	4/2	7/62	32,911
GEORGIA TECH	44	25	172	293	30/19	1	5/0	2/20	Home
South Carolina	6	13	40	156	32/15	3	2/2	4/28	46,011
GEORGIA TECH	27	17	210	136	20/11	2	3/2	7/55	Home
GEORGIA TECH	31	23	202	276	24/15	0	2/1	7/43	31,941
Maryland	3	13	-20	255	42/20	2	0/0	5/30	Away
Clemson	19	21	290	53	14/3	1	2/1	5/35	46,066
GEORGIA TECH	21	9	74	144	17/10	1	1/1	5/25	Home
Georgia Tech	13	24	252	103	28/13	2	4/2	4/20	48,000
North Carolina	13	9	103	48	20/8	0	0/0	3/26	Away
Duke	31	23	84	291	52/27	1	2/1	11/90	44,061
GEORGIA TECH	48	20	316	92	19/10	1	0/0	8/48	Home
GEORGIA TECH	41	27	206	257	29/17	1	0/0	7/51	49,700
Virginia	38	21	168	344	28/18	2	1/1	6/44	Away
Virginia Tech	3	14	110	230	24/12	3	2/2	4/30	43,011
GEORGIA TECH	6	24	161	199	33/19	2	2/1	5/44	Home
GEORGIA TECH	42	22	344	108	16/8	2	4/1	2/20	13,493
Wake Forest	7	17	84	262	40/20	4	4/3	2/15	Away
GEORGIA TECH	40	24	216	225	20/15	0	2/1	6/65	82,122
Georgia	23	18	131	148	18/10	1	2/1	8/52	Away
Nebraska	21	14	126	209	25/14	0	3/2	6/69	72,328
GEORGIA TECH	45	19	190	277	23/16	1	2/1	5/50	Citrus Bowl

LETTERMEN

LETTERMEN RETURNING (48)

OFFENSE (27)
Split End: EMMETT MERCHANT, Brent Goolsby, David Stegall, Jason McGill
Flanker: BOBBY RODRIGUEZ, Greg Lester, Keenan Walker
Tight End: TOM COVINGTON, Derek Goshay, Anthony Rice
Tackle: MIKE MOONEY, Chris Brooks, Russell Freeman, Woodie Milam, Jim Kushon
Guard: John Lewis, Kyle Frederick, Scott Gold, James MacKendree**
Center: BILLY CHUBBS, Stacy Parker
Quarterback: SHAWN JONES, Jeff Howard
Fullback: Jeff Wright
Running Back: Kevin Tisdel
Placekicker: SCOTT SISSON, Alan Waters

DEFENSE (21)
Outside Linebacker: MARCO COLEMAN, MARLON WILLIAMS, Tom Johnson, Steve Pharr*
Defensive Tackle: COLEMAN RUDOLPH, Jim Gallagher, Richard Kimsey
Noseguard: KEVIN BATTLE, Bryan Baxter
Inside Linebacker: JERRELLE WILLIAMS, Erick Fry, Darrell Swilling
Cornerback: WILLIE CLAY, CURLEY DAY, Marcus Coleman, Mike Williams, Frank Scott
Safety: KEN SWILLING, Eric Bellamy, Kevin Peoples
Punter: Bill Weaver

*Lettered at Inside Linebacker in 1990
**Lettered at Tight End in 1989 and 1990

LETTERMEN LOST (28)

OFFENSE (15)
Split End: Terry Pettis
Flanker: Jerry Gilchrist, Randy Dollar
Tackle: DARRYL JENKINS
Guard: JOE SIFFRI, JIM LAVIN, Mark Hutto
Center: Veryl Miller
Quarterback: Paul Bowman
Fullback: STEFEN SCOTTON, Carl Lawson, James Reese
Running Back: WILLIAM BELL, T. J. Edwards
Placekicker: James Merritt

DEFENSE (13)
Outside Linebacker: Chris Simmons, Orion Cox
Defensive Tackle: JERIMIAH MCCLARY
Inside Linebacker: CALVIN TIGGLE, Rich Strohmeier, Scott Travis#
Cornerback: Keith Holmes, Angelo Rush
Safety: THOMAS BALKCOM, Jay Martin, Chris Allen
Punter: SCOTT ALDREDGE, Tony Gariety

#Out for 1991 season due to knee injury

1990 STARTING LINEUPS GAME-BY-GAME

OFFENSE

	N.C. State	UTC	S.C.	Maryland	Clemson	UNC	Duke	Virginia	Va. Tech	W. Forest	Georgia	Nebraska
SE	Merchant	Merchant	Merchant	Merchant	Merchant	Merchant	Merchant	Merchant	Merchant	Merchant	Merchant	Merchant
LT	Jenkins	Jenkins	Jenkins	Jenkins	Jenkins	Jenkins	Jenkins	Jenkins	Jenkins	Jenkins	Jenkins	Jenkins
LG	Lavin	Lavin	Lavin	Lavin	Lavin	Lavin	Lavin	Lavin	Lavin	Lavin	Lavin	Lavin
C	Chubbs	Miller	Chubbs	Miller	Chubbs	Miller	Chubbs	Miller	Chubbs	Chubbs	Miller	Miller
RG	Siffri	Siffri	Siffri	Siffri	Siffri	Siffri	Siffri	Siffri	Siffri	Siffri	Siffri	Siffri
RT	Mooney	Mooney	Mooney	Mooney	Mooney	Freeman	Mooney	Mooney	Mooney	Mooney	Mooney	Mooney
TE	Covington	Covington	Covington	Covington	Covington	Covington	Covington	Covington	Covington	Covington	Covington	Covington
QB	Jones	Jones	Jones	Jones	Jones	Jones	Jones	Jones	Jones	Jones	Jones	Jones
FB	Scotton	Scotton	Scotton	Scotton	Scotton	Rice*	Scotton	Goshay*	Scotton	Scotton	Scotton	Scotton
RB	Bell	Bell	Bell	Edwards	Edwards	Bell	Bell	Bell	Bell	Bell	Bell	Bell
FL	Rodriguez	Lester	Rodriguez	Lester	Rodriguez	Rodriguez	Rodriguez	Rodriguez	Gilchrist	Rodriguez	Rodriguez	Rodriguez
K	Sisson	Sisson	Sisson	Sisson	Sisson	Sisson	Sisson	Sisson	Sisson	Sisson	Sisson	Sisson

*Two tight ends, no fullback in opening alignment

DEFENSE

	N.C. State	UTC	S.C.	Maryland	Clemson	UNC	Duke	Virginia	Va. Tech	W. Forest	Georgia	Nebraska
OLB	MoColeman	MoColeman	MoColeman	MoColeman	MoColeman	MoColeman	MoColeman	MoColeman	Simmons	MoColeman	MoColeman	MoColeman
DT	Rudolph	Rudolph	Rudolph	Rudolph	Rudolph	Rudolph	Rudolph	Rudolph	Rudolph	Rudolph	Rudolph	Rudolph
NG	Battle	Battle	Battle	Battle	Battle	Battle	Battle	Battle	Battle	Battle	Battle	Battle
DT	McClary	McClary	McClary	McClary	McClary	McClary	McClary	McClary	McClary	McClary	McClary	McClary
OLB	M.Williams	M.Williams	M.Williams	M.Williams	M.Williams	M.Williams	M.Williams	M.Williams	M.Williams	M.Williams	M.Williams	M.Williams
ILB	J.Williams	J.Williams	J.Williams	J.Williams	J.Williams	J.Williams	J.Williams	J.Williams	J.Williams	J.Williams	J.Williams	J.Williams
ILB	Tiggle	Tiggle	Tiggle	Tiggle	Tiggle	Tiggle	Tiggle	Tiggle	Tiggle	Tiggle	Tiggle	Tiggle
BC	Day	Holmes	Holmes	Holmes	Holmes	Holmes	Holmes	Holmes	Day	Day	Day	Day
FC	Clay	Clay	Clay	Clay	Clay	Clay	Clay	Clay	Clay	Clay	Clay	Clay
SS	Balkcom	Balkcom	Balkcom	Balkcom	Balkcom	Balkcom	Balkcom	Balkcom	Balkcom	Balkcom	Balkcom	Balkcom
FS	K.Swilling	K.Swilling	K.Swilling	K.Swilling	Bellamy	Martin	Martin	K.Swilling	K.Swilling	K.Swilling	K.Swilling	K.Swilling
P	Aldredge	Aldredge	Aldredge	Aldredge	Aldredge	Aldredge	Aldredge	Aldredge	Aldredge	Aldredge	Aldredge	Aldredge

SUPERLATIVES

1990 GEORGIA TECH FOOTBALL SUPERLATIVES
Does Not Include Florida Citrus Bowl

Individual Bests

Longest run from scrimmage: 52 yards, William Bell vs. Duke

Longest TD run: 26 yards, Shawn Jones vs. North Carolina

Longest pass completion: 78 yards, Shawn Jones to William Bell vs. Tennessee-Chattanooga (TD)

Longest TD pass: 78 yards, Shawn Jones to William Bell vs. UT-Chattanooga

Longest field goal: 43 yards, Scott Sisson vs. Duke

Longest punt: 54 yards, Scott Aldredge vs. Maryland

Longest punt return: 26 yards, Willie Clay vs. Clemson

Longest kickoff return: 87 yards, Kevin Tisdel vs. Clemson (85 yds. for TD vs. Duke)

Longest interception return: 83 yards, Michael Williams vs. Wake Forest (TD)

Most rushing carries: 24, William Bell vs. Georgia

Most rushing yards: 166, William Bell vs. Duke

Most pass attempts: 33, Shawn Jones vs. Virginia Tech

Most pass completions: 19, Shawn Jones vs. Virginia Tech

Most passing yards: 276, Shawn Jones vs. Maryland (15 completions, 24 attempts)

Most receptions: 6, Bobby Rodriguez vs. Georgia (119 yards, 2 TD)

Most receiving yards: 119, Bobby Rodriguez vs. Georgia (6 rec.)

Most total yards: 309, Shawn Jones vs. Virginia (35 plays, 257 passing, 52 rushing)

Most touchdowns: 2, William Bell vs. UTC, Jeff Wright vs. Maryland, Shawn Jones vs. Duke, Stefen Scotton vs. Duke, Jerry Gilchrist vs. Virginia, Bobby Rodriguez vs. Wake Forest and Georgia

Most points scored: 14, Scott Sisson vs. Tennessee-Chattanooga

Most rushing TDs: 2, Jeff Wright vs. Maryland, Shawn Jones vs. Duke, Stefen Scotton vs. Duke

Most receiving TDs: 2, Bobby Rodriguez vs. Georgia

Most points kicking: 14, Scott Sisson vs. UT-Chattanooga (3 field goals, 5 PATs)

Best punting average: 44.0 yards, Scott Aldredge vs. N.C. State (7 punts)

Most total tackles: 24, Calvin Tiggle vs. Clemson

Most interceptions: 2, Ken Swilling vs. South Carolina, Willie Clay vs. Virginia Tech

Longest Tech scoring drive: 94 yards vs. Maryland (6 plays, 2:11 time elapsed)

Longest opponent scoring drive: 80 yards by Virginia (3 plays, 1:26 time elapsed)

Last shutout by Tech defense: Oct. 15, 1988 vs. South Carolina (34-0)

Consecutive scoring games by Tech: 40 (last time shut out, 17-0 at N.C. State, Oct. 3, 1987)

Team Offensive Highs and Lows

Points Scored	48, Duke	6, Va. Tech
First Downs	27, Virginia	9, Clemson
Rushing	18, Wake Forest	3, Clemson
Passing	14, Virginia	3, W. Forest
Rushing Yards	344, Wake Forest	74, Clemson
Passing Yards	293, UTC	92, Duke
Total Offense	478, Maryland	218, Clemson
Offensive Plays	87, Virginia Tech	49, Clemson
Rushing Attempts	57, Wake Forest	32, Clemson
Pass Attempts	33, Virginia Tech	16, W. Forest
Pass Completions	19, Virginia Tech	8, W. Forest
Had Intercepted	0, Maryland, Ga.	2, S. Carolina, N. Carolina, Va. Tech, Wake Forest
Fumbles Lost	0, UTC, Duke, UVa.	3, N.C. State
Penalty Yards	6, N.C. State	65, Georgia
Time of Possession	36:45, Va. Tech	21:50, Clemson
QB Sacks Allowed	0, Md., Clemson, Duke, Georgia, Wake Forest, Virginia	4, N.C. State,

Team Defensive Highs and Lows

Points Allowed	3, Md., Va. Tech	38, Virginia
First Downs	9, N. Carolina	23, Duke
Rushing	1, Maryland	18, Clemson
Passing	1, N. Carolina	15, Duke
Rushing Yards	(minus-20) vs. Md.	290, Clemson
Passing Yards	48, N. Carolina	344, Virginia
Total Offense	151, N. Carolina	512, Virginia
Offensive Plays	54, Virginia Tech	89, Clemson
Rushing Attempts	25, Maryland	75, Clemson
Passing Attempts	14, Clemson	52, Duke
Pass Completions	3, Clemson	27, Duke
Pass Interceptions	5, UTC	0, N. Carolina
Fumbles Recovered	3, N.C. State, Wake	0, Md., UNC
Quarterback Sacks	11, Maryland	0, Virginia